# WHO KNOWS

# WHO KNOWS
## Knowledge According to Spiritual Philosophy

Nirushan Sivanesan

© Nirushan Sivanesan 2024

Text copyright © Nirushan Sivanesan 2024
Cover Design copyright © Chrissie Yeomans 2024
All rights reserved.

Nirushan Sivanesan has asserted his right under the Copyright, Designs and Patents Act 1988 to be identified as the author of this work.

No part of this book may be reprinted or reproduced or utilised in any form or by electronic, mechanical or any other means, now known or hereafter invented, including photocopying or recording, or in any information storage or retrieval system, without the permission in writing from the Publisher and Author.

First published 2024
by Rowanvale Books Ltd
The Gate
Keppoch Street
Roath
Cardiff
CF24 3JW
www.rowanvalebooks.com

A CIP catalogue record for this book is available from the British Library.
ISBN: 978-1-83584-006-1
E-Book ISBN: 978-1-83584-005-4

*Every now and then a man's mind is stretched by a new idea or sensation, and never shrinks back to its former dimensions.*

- Oliver Wendell Holmes Sr.

# CONTENTS

## PART 1 –
## THE PROBLEM OF GENERAL PHILOSOPHY

Introduction to Epistemology ................................................... 9
The Limitation of Knowledge .................................................. 18
Psychological Bias – External Factors ..................................... 24
Psychological Bias – Internal Factors ...................................... 35
Theism Versus Atheism ........................................................... 44

## PART 2 –
## THE SOLUTION BY SPIRITUAL PHILOSOPHY

The Beginning of Spirituality .................................................. 50
The Criteria for Spirituality ..................................................... 58
Why Some Believe and Others Don't ...................................... 65
The Case for the Non-natural .................................................. 75
The Message of Spiritual Philosophy ...................................... 81

*Index* ....................................................................................... 91

# PART 1 –
# THE PROBLEM OF GENERAL PHILOSOPHY

## Introduction to Epistemology

Put simply, ontology is the study of what exists. Epistemology is the study of how we acquire knowledge of that which exists. So ontology deals with what there *is* to know, and epistemology deals with *how* to know it.

But do you need to first know what there is to know (and then how to know it), or do you need to first know how to know (and then, from this, deduce what there is to know)? This dilemma gives rise to the questions: *How* do you know what exists (an epistemological problem for ontology)? And *what*, if anything, is the object of knowledge (an ontological problem for epistemology)?

You have to apply an epistemological method to know what there is to know (what exists); so epistemology has to precede ontology. But epistemology requires a focus of knowledge—there has to be *something* that it attempts to know (i.e. you have to claim something exists and then work out how to know it); so ontology has to precede epistemology. Thus the two disciplines rely on each other in a manner that creates a chicken-or-egg dilemma[1]. And

---

[1] The chicken-or-egg dilemma, arising from the question "did the chicken or the egg come first?", reveals a problem of causation when two things need each other to exist: As you can only get a chicken from an egg but need a chicken to lay an egg, neither can be first.

this demonstrates the peculiarity of acquiring knowledge. But let's put this to one side for now and revisit it later.

Ontology, as a matter of course, investigates and deals with the non-physical aspects of reality—it addresses questions that go beyond the physical world and beyond physical investigation, such as the existence of numbers, God, souls, and moral truths. But ontology is a contentious subject, as some people think there isn't anything beyond physics and the physical world (and that even if there is, it can never be known to exist). Consequently, the philosophical discourse in ontology is littered with implacable disputes and has not hitherto yielded a consensus in any of its major branches of enquiry: characteristically, one group affirms the existence of some object (realists), while another rejects the existence of said object (antirealists).

Epistemology investigates and deals with the methods used to gain either knowledge of the non-physical reality (if such exists) or knowledge of the nature and operations of the physical world. However, current philosophical thinking generally considers there to be no adequate means by which a non-physical reality and metaphysical claims can be known.[2] Traditionally, in the philosophy of epistemology, there are three means by which knowledge is acquired: experience, reason, and intuition. All knowledge supposedly comes through one of these means.

Experience is perception of the physical universe. This occurs when one of the sense organs (eyes, ears, nose, tongue, or skin) is occupied with one of the sense modalities (sight, sound, smell, taste, or touch). Such perceptions give rise to knowledge of the objects and operations of the universe. Experience also refers to

---

[2] Metaphysics can be considered the study that deals with the existence and the nature of things. Ontology is a sub-field of metaphysics, as metaphysics encompasses more general questions about the fundamental nature of reality.

knowledge derived from memory and testimony. However, testimony is typically transmitted through the written word or orally (i.e. it is seen or heard), and memories are the result of previous perceptual experiences; thus both memory and testimony can be considered forms of perceptual experience. (Knowledge derived from perceptual experience is termed "empirical knowledge", and *empiricism* is the view that empirical knowledge is the most reliable source of knowledge.)

Science and the scientific method are based on empirical knowledge but *also* require repeatable observations, experimentation, and testing. Thus all science is empirical knowledge but not all empirical knowledge is science (like, all poodles are dogs but not all dogs are poodles). For instance, if you eat an apple, you learn of its taste: you have acquired empirical knowledge of the apple, but this knowledge is not a result of the scientific method, as you don't need to repeat the experience to prove the knowledge. Similarly, if you witness a murder, you have acquired empirical knowledge of that murder: of course, the murder cannot be repeated to corroborate your knowledge. And if people testify to an incident, you have acquired empirical knowledge of that incident without having applied a scientific methodology: this is an example of oral transmission where knowledge is *heard* by you but not obtained through the scientific method or direct experience. (*Scientism* is the view that science is the most reliable source of knowledge.)

Reason is the process of using the rational capacities of our minds to draw logical inferences. It relies on the laws of logic (which must be considered fundamental axiomatic truths for logic, and consequently reason, to function).[3] But even though reason

---

[3] An axiom (or axiomatic truth) is a proposition that is accepted as true without the need for justification, usually without controversy. Axioms form the foundation of an argument or a discipline.

relies on logic, reason must be used to *know* logic. So reason gives rise to knowledge of logic (and, by way of inference, mathematics too): for example, "2 + 2 = 4" is theoretical knowledge that arises in the human mind through analytic reasoning; it does not rely on sense experience of the physical universe. (*Rationalism* is the view that reason is the most reliable source of knowledge.)

Logical reasoning is based on deduction (deductive reasoning) and is often presented as a syllogism. For example:

| | |
|---|---|
| a) All swans are white; | [premise] |
| b) Toby is a swan; | [premise] |
| c) Therefore Toby is white. | [conclusion] |

In this example, reason alone provides the knowledge that Toby is white, and there is no need to perceive Toby. Such conclusions are considered necessarily true if the premises are true.

The first thing to check with such a syllogism is that the conclusion logically follows from the premises (i.e. it is "deductively valid"). In this case, it does. But if statement *c* was "Toby is black", then clearly the conclusion would be an illogical one, i.e. a deductively invalid syllogism. But note, the conclusion *could* still be true (i.e. Toby could be black)—a conclusion can be deductively invalid but true.

The second thing to check is that the premises are true. If they are not, the conclusion is not necessarily true—a conclusion can be deductively valid but false (if a premise is false). For instance, statement *a* could be false (perhaps some swans are black), or statement *b* could be false (perhaps Toby is actually a goose), meaning that the argument (not the deduction) would be wrong, and therefore the conclusion is not necessarily true (Toby is not necessarily white). But note, even if a premise is false, this does not mean the conclusion is necessarily untrue (Toby could indeed be white).

Thus a proposed syllogism can be one of four things: valid with a true conclusion, valid with a false conclusion, invalid with a true conclusion, or invalid with a false conclusion.

In fact, this is relevant in psychiatry. Delusional beliefs in psychosis are diagnosed only if they have been deduced illogically—whether they are true or not is irrelevant. The classic example used to highlight this is the belief that a spouse is having an affair: if a person believes this solely because it is raining more than usual, then the belief is delusional (regardless of whether the spouse is having an affair or not), as their reasoning is illogical.

Intuition is knowledge that arises in a person without any analytic reasoning, through means such as "gut-feelings" (instinct), extrasensory perceptions (psychic abilities or the "sixth sense"), or prophecy (Divine revelation). Thus intuition can be described as an inexplicable inner sense that a particular proposition is true. Western philosophy, however, typically disregards intuition and renders it an unreliable source of knowledge...

The Enlightenment period of Western Europe cultivated the idea that all knowledge should be supported by reason and/or empirical means, a view labelled *logical empiricism* (or *logical positivism*). And this position appears to be the current paradigm—only claims that are verifiable through direct observation or logical proof can constitute true or justified knowledge, i.e. if you can't perceive it or reason it, then you can't know it or claim it as true.

But, in actual fact, there is no means by which a hierarchy of these epistemological methods can be determined. It is all just personal preference. So one is not wrong to claim that intuition is a better source of knowledge than reason is, as there is no way of disproving this claim without relying on reason: to use reason to argue for reason is a form of circular reasoning.[4] Similarly, empiricism is merely an unjustified assertion (more on this in a moment) and thus there is no epistemic justification to conclude that reason or perceptual experience is more reliable than intuition as a source of knowledge. Also, intuition is self-evident as a source of knowledge—there are things that you just know without any justification or explanation. I will justify this claim in a moment, but before I do, it is worth clarifying the distinction between intuition and perception...

Perception is when one of your sense organs conveys information about the physical universe to you. (Note, a true perception is linked to an external physical stimulus; if the stimulus is non-physical, then the perception is a hallucination.) Whereas, intuition is when information about the physical universe *or* non-physical matters (if such exist) arises within you through non-perceptual means. (This may include hallucinations.)

(Hallucinations are generally considered representative of psychopathology. For instance, visual and auditory hallucinations are associated with schizophrenia, as they are assumed to represent phenomena that aren't really there or don't exist in reality. But how do we know they don't really exist? Well, if someone sees or hears something that nobody else can see or hear, then people typically presume that it doesn't really exist. It may, however, be the case that it does exist and only this one person can perceive it. Thus when I use the term hallucination, I am not ascribing any truth value to it [it may or may not represent a true phenomenon] and am merely saying that it is a perception without an external physical stimulus. Of note, society does tend to recognise

---

4 Circular reasoning (also known as "begging the question" or "question begging") is a logical fallacy whereby the conclusion of an argument is used as a premise of that same argument.

a distinction between schizophrenic hallucinations [which society says do not represent true phenomena] and religious visions or auditions [which society says might represent true phenomena]: however, there is no clear methodology for making this distinction.)

As a side note, there is also the phenomenon of internal perception. This gives you knowledge about your own body through feelings like hunger and pain. These are not sensory experiences, as they are not dependent on external perceptual stimuli; they are feelings that arise internally and inform you of a state of affairs in your body. Consequently, you acquire the knowledge that your body is hungry or that part of your body is creating pain. For instance, when you fall over and break your leg, an external stimulus creates a perception in your touch sense that forms the initial knowledge that there is damage to your leg. But continued pain from your leg, which gives you the knowledge that there is a problem, is not a sense perception, as a true perception can only arise from an external stimulus. (There is no continuous external stimulus in this instance—the fall is in the past.) Similarly, if you have a heart attack, various symptoms such as pain, dizziness, and nausea inform you that there is a problem in your heart—this is knowledge that does not come from external stimuli or your sense organs.[5] Both rationalists and empiricists may argue that, even though such bodily feelings can result in knowledge of one's own internal system, they cannot produce knowledge of the physical universe. But take the example of food poisoning: severe

---

5 The sense organ for touch perception is said to be the skin, in the same way the eyes are for sight, the ears are for hearing, the nose is for smell, and the tongue is for taste. Touch consists of several distinct sensations (pain, temperature, pressure, and vibration), but all of these are related to external stimuli interacting with the skin. Internal feelings of pain, and other bodily feelings, are not due to touch perception.

abdominal cramps, nausea, vomiting, and diarrhoea (which are *not* perceptual experiences) can tell you that a particular food is contaminated, and this knowledge can then be used to alert others, so it has practical value. In this example, you are not processing sensory perceptions into knowledge but bodily feelings into knowledge—the knowledge of the food being contaminated, which pertains to the physical universe, is *not* acquired solely through empirical means and logic.

Back to the issue at hand... What knowledge arises from intuition?

Well, how do you know that someone loves you? This, you just intuitively know. Some may argue that you use reason and perception to conclude that someone loves you. And it is difficult to disprove such a hypothesis, as it can be argued that your mind determines whether someone loves you through various logical deductions, such as how the person behaves with you. But it seems that there is a connection on a deeper level which determines such a conclusion. This is said to be the soul's instinctive interaction with another, which can be likened to two magnets attracting each other—an invisible force that is not based in reason or sense experience. This is the idea that you can just *feel* an instant connection to someone: the so-called soulmate.

And some think that moral intuitions reflect objective moral truths; as objective moral truths cannot be observed or reasoned, they can only be intuited or revealed (if they exist).[6] (Note, we make a distinction here between knowledge derived through personal intuition and knowledge derived through external

---

[6] Some moral philosophers, most notably Immanuel Kant (a German philosopher born in 1724), have claimed that objective morality is known through reasoning. However, this view is typically dismissed and can be considered the "is-ought" problem of moral philosophy, as first described by David Hume (an 18th Century Scottish philosopher). (See my other title *The Moral Law* for more on this.)

revelation, even though both are categorised under the umbrella term of "intuition".)

Also, all scientific hypotheses have to start with a spark of creativity that cannot be justified or explained through reason or sense experience, otherwise a regress problem occurs. That is, if all ideas have to come from previous experiences and reasoning, then how do the first ideas transpire?

And people can just intuit something without any specific reasoning—they just *feel* it and can't explain or justify it with evidence (perceptual experiences) or reason (deductive arguments), but "know" it to be true. *Where* such knowledge comes from is debatable, but some claim it comes from a process that has recently become known as "morphic resonance".[7]

For instance, I once played online chess against an old friend, and at the start was beating him easily. Though, a few days later he played much better and beat me. At the time I congratulated him and was impressed. But later that day, a thought struck me: "He is cheating." I don't know where this thought came from, and I didn't reason my way to it; it just appeared and I resonated with it, and it *felt* true, yet I had no evidence to support it. But I then went looking for said evidence. I analysed our games and noticed features that were consistent with cheating by use of a chess "bot". Consequently, I built a case against him, and he confessed when confronted with it.

Now, taking credit for "working this out" would be a mistake, as *I* didn't work anything out. The knowledge just sprung forth within me. Inexplicably. And this represents the phenomenon of

---

[7] Morphic resonance (a term coined by the contemporary British biologist Rupert Sheldrake) denotes mysterious telepathy-type interconnections between organisms that can account for strange phenomena, such as thinking of someone just before they call you or knowing that someone is staring at you without seeing them do so. Such knowledge is not derived through experience or reason.

"knowledge" arising within a person through some mysterious process. But such methods are typically dismissed by Western philosophy, and, in psychiatry, such knowledge may be considered delusional and lead to involuntary detention and treatment! So the current paradigm does not permit "unjustified" knowledge claims; you are not allowed to make knowledge claims unless you can back them up with some kind of evidence or reasoning.

Interestingly, we played again a few months later, and the same pattern emerged, resulting in the same intuitive feeling that he was cheating. I once again built a case against him, which was based on more or less the same evidence. But this time, lo and behold, he proved his innocence and that I was wrong, meaning the same evidence and same feeling had given rise, on this second occasion, to an untrue belief. So internal convictions based on gut-feelings can be wrong too; there is no fundamental law that says intuition reflects reality. However, spiritual philosophy explains the relationship between intuitions and knowledge, and we will explore this later.

## The Limitation of Knowledge

Spiritual philosophy makes a distinction between higher knowledge and lower knowledge. The Upanishads, which form part of the Hindu scriptures, enunciate this: higher knowledge refers to knowledge of the fundamental reality, which is known as *Brahman* in Hindu thought and God (or the Father) in Christian thought; lower knowledge refers to knowledge pertaining to the external world, including logic, mathematics, and the sciences. However, you can never know anything about the external world with certainty, and therefore all lower knowledge is fallible. This is because all knowledge boils down, or regresses, into unjustifiable axioms or presuppositions. Recognition and acceptance of this can lead to a position of factual relativism (truth is relative) or epistemological nihilism (truth can never be known). These positions are associated with global scepticism.

The Munchhausen trilemma is a philosophical thought experiment that demonstrates the impossibility of proving any truth, including in the fields of logic and mathematics, by establishing that all knowledge claims regress into one of three possibilities: a circular argument, an infinite regress, or a dogma. So there is question begging with any and every ideology, philosophical worldview, or belief system. In view of this, all lower knowledge is subjective, as it requires the subjective acceptance of an unprovable axiom. And this acceptance is, as I will justify shortly, based on psychological disposition, meaning such "knowledge" is essentially built on personal preference or, what can be described as, "faith". Seemingly, the ancient Greek philosopher Socrates acknowledged this when he said, *"I know that I know nothing"*, implying that no one can know anything, and thus the person who thinks he knows something is unwise.

Reason cannot give you certain knowledge, as there is no fundamental law in operation that says reason reflects reality. For instance, even if it's somehow shown that belief in God is irrational, that does not entail that God does not exist—irrationality does not necessarily equal untruth. Also, all logic and mathematics are based on unjustified and unprovable axioms, and thus can be questioned. Even the fundamental laws of logic can be, and have been, argued against.[8] Similarly, "2 + 2 = 4" is only true if you accept certain axioms, and thus can be argued to be false. So you have to adopt a faith in these axioms to practise

---

8 There are three classical fundamental laws of logic: (1) the law of identity – each thing is identical to itself; (2) the law of non-contradiction – no proposition is true and untrue at the same time; (3) the law of excluded middle – either a proposition or its negation is true.

logic or mathematics, as you cannot know for sure that they are true. Furthermore, some argue that, if evolution is true, then we have evolved to survive, not to know the truth; hence there are no grounds to think that our reason has evolved to inform us of the truth, and perhaps instead it has evolved to give us false beliefs that aid our survival.

Sensory experience cannot give you certain knowledge either, as how do you know that your sense perceptions are reliable? Perhaps you are hallucinating and thus your perceptual experiences do not in fact reflect reality. Or perhaps you are perceiving an illusion; this world could be a mirage (a phenomenon that is perceived correctly but represents an unreality). Or perhaps you are dreaming; a dream seems very real during the dream, but once you wake, you realise that the experience was an unreality created by your mind—this waking state could similarly be an unreality created by your mind.

René Descartes, a French philosopher born in 1596, was cognisant of this issue. He argued that experience cannot lead to certain knowledge, as one cannot be sure that their sense perceptions are reflecting reality. To validate this idea, Descartes produced a thought experiment of an Evil Demon who creates and presents an illusory external world in order to deceive us—our experiences would be unreal and we'd be living in an unreality but wouldn't know it. There is seemingly no way of disproving such a hypothesis, so it is always a possibility. (I say "seemingly" because spiritual philosophy offers a way of disproving this, as I will demonstrate later.)

Descartes concluded that, as long as the Evil Demon is possible, we cannot trust any of our beliefs and thus cannot know anything. Because, all our perceptual experiences (or even thoughts) could have come from the Evil Demon's illusion (or been implanted in our minds by him): we would have no way of negating this or distinguishing the unreality from the reality (unless the Evil Demon somehow revealed this knowledge to us). This led Descartes to global scepticism and the idea that he could not know anything and that he should doubt everything ("Cartesian doubt"). The philosophy of scepticism, and subsequently fallibilism, are largely attributed to these ideas from Descartes. (Gilbert Harman's "brain in a vat" thought experiment is a contemporary version of Descartes' Evil Demon idea.)[9]

However, Descartes realised that there was *one* thing he did know: he knew he was doubting. And he realised that for there to be a doubt, there must be a doubter, and for there to be a thought, there must be a thinker. Consequently, Descartes confirmed his own existence, and thought it indubitable to proclaim "I exist". That is to say, "I am a conscious entity having a conscious experience, and therefore must exist in some form or the other". From this realisation, he developed what is known as the *Cogito*, which represents the Latin statement *"Cogito Ergo Sum"*—"I think therefore I am".

Moving on... Science, or the scientific method, primarily relies on induction (the process of producing hypotheses from general observations). And the main purpose of science is to offer an explanation (a model of causation) for phenomena and observations, which can then be used to make testable predictions. Of note, induction is based on the principle that fundamental laws

---

9 The "brain in a vat" thought experiment, by contemporary American philosopher Gilbert Harman, suggests that your existence, as you experience it, is a deception: your brain has been removed from your body and placed in a vat where it is connected to a supercomputer which transmits electrical impulses identical to those that a brain normally receives. Thus the computer simulates reality, making you believe that certain things are happening that aren't actually happening, not outside your own realm of consciousness anyway. The simulation requires an architect, and this is hypothesised to be a mad scientist who is carrying out the experiment for unknown reasons. As such, technically speaking, the mad scientist is the creator of everything. Or rather, he has made *you* the creator of everything, as everything originates from your brain. Like Descartes' Evil Demon, there are no conventional means by which this hypothesis can be disproven.

are constant and things behave in the same way. For instance, our observations have shown that the sun has risen every day, so science predicts that the sun will rise tomorrow.

David Hume, an 18th Century Scottish philosopher, recognised a problem with induction. He claimed that you cannot know for certain that things will behave in the same way, and therefore your hypotheses can never be proven certain. He gave the example of a chicken that is visited and fed by a farmer every day until one day the farmer comes to wring its neck. The chicken, or an observer, would have been wrong to presume that the farmer would continue to feed it until it dies of natural causes. This problem with induction is also demonstrated by the black swan fallacy: it was once thought in Europe that all swans were white, as all known swans were white, but this hypothesis was later falsified by the observation of black swans in Australia. So induction cannot lead to certain knowledge; even though the sun has risen every day so far, this does not necessitate that the sun will rise tomorrow.

Hume also recognised a problem with causation. He identified that it is never possible to know the cause of an event. Two events can be correlated, and we can observe two events occurring in sequence, but we can never observe the cause. He gave the example of one billiard ball hitting another. It feels natural to conclude that the first ball impacting with the second is the cause of motion in the second ball, but even if we were observing this as an experiment, we never actually *see* the motion in the first ball *cause* the second ball to move. All we see are two separate events, and we cannot see nor prove the connection between them—there is no sensory impression of causation even though there are sensory impressions of the events themselves. (You can know something by seeing it; you can know the colour blue by seeing it, but you can never see causation, so it is not knowable through empirical means [knowledge obtained through sense experience].)

Hume's conclusions from these ideas are debated amongst philosophers. Some think that Hume refutes causation, claiming that there are just sequences of events that are in "constant conjunction" (always correlated), and that is all that can be said about them—it cannot be said that A *causes* B, but it can be said that whenever A happens, B follows. A second view is that Hume thinks people project causation onto the world—the human mind observes a sequence of events and creates an impression of necessary connection thereby imposing a causal structure on the world. And a third view is that Hume accepts causation, or necessary connection, but asserts that there is no way of detecting it.

This idea is also present in Hindu philosophy and was descriptively brought out in the Yoga Vasistha, an ancient Hindu scripture. In this, the analogy is given of a crow landing on a palm tree just as a coconut from that tree falls to the ground. An inference is then made by the observer that the crow landing on the tree directly caused the coconut to fall. These two events, however, may not be causally related but just coincidence, or related in a subtler manner. Perhaps the crow senses when a coconut is just about to fall from a branch, through means we do not know, and then chooses to land on such a branch, again for reasons we do not know: (perhaps the crow likes the sound of a coconut landing on the ground or perhaps it is signalling to other organisms that there will soon be an edible coconut underneath it). These are not inconceivable ideas and therefore cannot be ruled out. So to conclude that one event has led to the other is an unprovable assumption.

For centuries, farmers have observed the behavioural patterns of insects to predict weather. And it is said that spiders-in-motion precedes rain. However, we cannot say that spiders-in-motion is the *cause* of rain; just because one event precedes the other, it does not mean that it causes it. But at least we derive knowledge from this correlation (the knowledge that spiders move before rain and the knowledge that our sense faculties can detect moving spiders before they can detect rain), and there is predictive and practical value in the correlation: farmers can prepare for rain on observing moving spiders. Similarly, there is a correlation between lung cancer and smoking, resulting in the assumption that smoking *causes* lung cancer. But this could be wrong. Perhaps they are independent events, resulting from independent causes in the body, that simply arise in conjunction. Or perhaps lung cancer causes smoking: the lung cancer could exist far before the medical detection of it and give rise to urges to smoke, which then gives the false appearance of smoking preceding lung cancer. But the fact that there is a correlation can lead to modification in behaviour, and thus recognition of this correlation has some practical utility; whether it reflects causation or not is a metaphysical issue that cannot be proven.

## *Psychological Bias – External Factors*

The terms "belief" and "knowledge" should be used interchangeably, as all knowledge claims are beliefs. So separating them becomes arbitrary. And, as mentioned, faith is the underpinning of all beliefs and hence all knowledge claims too. But where does this faith come from and why do people believe what they believe?

The psychology of belief is a complex issue. But essentially, a person believes what they do based on various internal and external factors that give rise to psychological bias. External factors include their socio-cultural conditioning, and internal factors include their psychological disposition and inherent nature. (Although, these internal and external factors are, of course, inextricably linked and thus separating them is somewhat contentious.)

It is no surprise that the majority of people born in medieval Europe believed in the Christian God and the majority of people born in India at the same time believed in the Hindu Gods. And it's no surprise that the majority of people born and brought up in Western Europe today reject theism.

Consider this simple empirical question: is the Earth a globe? The answer that people give to this question is dependent on era and culture. Five hundred years ago, the majority of people in the West would have answered "no". Today, most educated people would answer "yes". But they cannot know this. And there are people who argue that the Earth is not a globe but a disc. Thus the decision to answer that it is a globe is based on psychological factors and not on reason or sense experience, as presumably the answerer has not flown into space and directly observed the shape of the Earth (and even if they had, they would then have to adopt faith in the reliability of their sense faculties).

If you believe that the Earth is a globe, you are adopting a faith. You are simply accepting what you are told and thus demonstrating trust and faith in the scientific establishment. You cannot know that the scientific establishment is correct. (In fact, historically, the scientific consensus has often been wrong.) Perhaps the scientific establishment is deliberately deceiving you for their own agenda. You may argue that such a position is conspiratorial, but you cannot disprove it, and therefore your belief in the claims that are dished out by the scientific establishment equate to faith.

If Socrates were alive today, he would probably respond with "I don't know" to this question, and this is the most intelligible answer that a person can give. Thus conspiracy theories and minority views should not be dismissed *ad lapidem*, but conversely, they shouldn't be accepted with strong conviction either. The best thing is to remain open-minded, as you cannot know which side is true. So you're better off walking around like

Socrates, claiming that you know nothing rather than claiming knowledge.

Regarding conspiracies, what is that factor that makes you believe the mainstream account over the conspiracy hypothesis? It can't be reason, because the conspiracist can provide logically valid arguments for their position. It can't be evidence, because the conspiracist can provide this too (and you probably have no means of testing it anyway). It seems that one of the main factors is *trust in the consensus*. But why trust the consensus over the minority? There is no logical argument to support such a position.

Note, we are not picking on science here. Religion has the same problem. Religious institutions similarly dish out dogma and then expect the masses to lap it up based on faith, which they often do, or at least *did* historically. But the difference is, the religionist (generally) recognises and accepts that faith is at the heart of his beliefs, whereas the science-follower claims that he does not resort to faith but reason and sense experience, which (for some unclear reason) he believes is an epistemically superior position. In reality, all he has done is swap the men in black robes for the men in white lab coats—whatever these men in white lab coats tell him, he laps it up.

A scientist might cite "the consensus" to justify his position, but there is no fundamental law that says the consensus reflects reality. And historically, the consensus, whether scientific or otherwise, has often been superseded. In fact, most of the major scientific theories in circulation today replaced previous consensuses. For instance, the heliocentric model for the solar system replaced the geocentric model, Einstein's theory of relativity replaced Newtonian mechanics, the germ theory of disease replaced the miasma theory of disease, and so on. Also, only a few decades ago, it was the majority scientific opinion that white people were inherently intellectually superior to non-white people, a conclusion formed on the back of "race science". Today, such a view is completely rejected by modern science.

Hence the majority does not determine what is right and wrong. Majority is not synonymous with truth. To believe in a scientific theory solely because the majority of scientists say that it is right, is a form of naivety and intellectual laziness. This can be appreciated by understanding the processes by which these scientific majorities are established...

When a scientific theory is proposed, it is put to the scientific community. This community is like a quiet audience that sits and listens to the speaker proposing his new ideology. As you can imagine, it's not just the actual scientific validity of the theory that counts, but multiple factors that affect the process of the theory being accepted or not: popularity of the speaker, marketing, secondary gain, to name a few. The theory may then be accepted by the scientific community, regardless of its viability. Once the theory is set in the scientific community, the "bandwagon effect" takes place. This is the phenomenon whereby people accept an ideology based on its popularity and jump on the bandwagon. The ideology then grows, as people opt to side with the consensus rather than analyse the case themselves. (These are the processes by which any new ideology is brought into the mainstream, including religious and political, and how an overwhelming acceptance of an unproven but popular idea can develop.)

For most people, it seems that fitting-in is more appealing than being different. If you're a scientist, you want to be part of the scientific community. In order to achieve this, you must accept what science tells you. It is not necessarily a case of deliberately accepting a fallacious theory for the purpose of self-preservation; it could merely be a case of psychological bias, whereby the desire to fit in and be part of the prestigious scientific community overpowers one's reason and draws them towards a certain ideology.

This is known as "herd mentality": people identify with a specific herd and then believe in any theory preached by that herd—they just go with the flow. From this, a "groupthink" situation arises wherein a specific group emerges and its members adopt a certain view and begin to think in the same way. Anyone who tries to challenge the view is cast outside the group. People outside the group are labelled outcasts and heretics and their opinions are ridiculed and considered unworthy. If you don't go with the party line, you can't be a member of the party: you are demoted to the backbenches.[10] People inside the group are encouraged to continue with the ideology and not question it or bring it into disrepute, which results in a loss of creativity and independent thinking. And once this ideology takes root in the scientific community, it is promoted and taught in the education system, thereby spreading amongst the non-scientific community through similar and other processes of indoctrination...

The desire to conform is a psychological trait that leads to belief in an ideology. The famous Asch Conformity Experiments from the 1950s revealed how social pressure from a majority group can lead a person to conform. In these experiments, an easy line judgement task was used: test subjects were given a pair of cards, one with a target line on it and the other with three lines of varying lengths, and then asked to match the target line to the correct line on the other card. The test was so easy that a near-100% correct response rate was expected (and, in fact, 99% was produced in the control study). However, these were group experiments in which actors were involved, and the test subjects were unaware of this. Each group was made up of multiple actors and only one

---

10 In UK politics, a backbencher is a member of parliament who is not given a role in the cabinet or shadow cabinet, and they have to sit quietly on the backbenches without having an influential role in the government/shadow government.

test subject, and participants had to read out their answers to the group, one by one; the actors were to go first and give incorrect answers, leaving the test subject to read out his answer last. The experiments found that, overall, about one-third of the read-aloud test responses were incorrect. And over the course of the trials, 75% of test subjects conformed at least once with the clearly incorrect majority, with only 25% consistently defying it. When the conforming test subjects were interviewed afterwards, they typically said that they conformed either because they wanted to be with the majority (normative influence) or because they thought the majority must be right and so doubted their own perceptions (informational influence). Solomon Asch, the creator of the study, said this about the results: *"That we have found the tendency to conformity in our society so strong that reasonably intelligent and well-meaning young people are willing to call white black is a matter of concern."*[11]

Hence the Asch experiments demonstrate that, for many people, conforming with majority opinion trumps reason and even trust in their own perceptions. And this enables any institution to indoctrinate its members (and society) with any ideology, and suggests that beliefs, whether scientific or religious, can form due to underlying psychological factors and not empirical evidence or reason (although these may be used after the fact to try and justify such a belief).

Consequently, a difficulty in changing a consensus-view arises... Once an ideology is dominant within a group, it becomes extremely difficult to dislodge it. Religious ideologies are obvious examples of this, but so too are scientific ones. Of course, scientific theories do change, but only within the parameters set by the scientific institution; one naturalistic explanation may be

---

11 Solomon E. Asch, "Opinions and Social Pressure," *Scientific American* 193 (1955): 34.

switched for another, but it will not be switched for a non-naturalistic explanation.[12]

As mentioned, the beliefs of an individual have complex causation and are inextricably intertwined with the beliefs of the collective. But the beliefs of the collective also have complex causation. Why and how paradigmatic beliefs change in a group are difficult to determine, but *actively* changing them is evidently nigh-on impossible. Thomas Kuhn, a 20th Century philosopher of science, recognised the phenomenon of "paradigm shifts" where a collective group takes on a new belief system. He was predominantly referring to scientific revolutions that cause a change in the scientific consensus; however, the phenomenon can be used to explain any change in ideology within a group.

For instance, five hundred years ago, Martin Luther triggered the Reformation with a written list of objections to Church doctrine. Legend has it that he nailed these to the door of a local church for the attention of the clergy, but instead a passer-by came across them, read them, and proceeded to print and circulate them to the masses. This led to a complete shift in religious attitude.

Now, we say "Martin Luther triggered" this shift, but actually we cannot know this, as Hume points out with his problem of causation—the two events are correlated, but this doesn't necessitate that one caused the other. Indeed, it is apparent that underlying psychological factors of the group must have been present for such a shift to happen; there must have been a collective yearning for this shift. And it seems reasonable to presume that this was caused by the masses waking up to the fallacy of Church doctrine,

---

12 Naturalism is a metaphysical philosophy that asserts that only natural (physical) laws and forces operate in the universe, and that nothing exists beyond the natural world. That is to say, there are no supernatural (non-physical) phenomena.

but perhaps there was also some animosity towards the Church due to all the atrocities it had committed (such as the burning of witches, the persecution of free-thinkers, the financial exploitation of the masses, and the advancement of religious wars), which would have understandably resulted in a psychological disposition to resist and reject any ideology or dogma espoused by the Church. Thus Martin Luther's objections are only the *seeming* cause; the true causation is probably much more complex and convoluted. But Luther's objections could be considered the catalyst that sparked the reaction and triggered the change. In this sense, an idea in itself may not be enough to create a paradigm shift; such a change may require a psychological yearning of the masses, perhaps triggered by a dissatisfaction with the status quo.

Though, one thing seems evident: change comes from *outside* the institution. Because, institutions are founded on a principle of self-preservation; they do not entertain ideas that threaten their own existence or the foundations upon which they are built. For instance, if a clergyman had opened that door and taken in Luther's list of objections before the public had the chance to access them, it seems likely that no change would have occurred—the change came from the people, not from the institution.

There are other sociological factors that also block such paradigm shifts. Traditionally, the written word via publication was the means by which new ideas were conveyed. Today, the spoken word through the media is also used. But these are run by institutions with their own agendas, such as self-preservation, political goals, or profit. If profit is the motive, then popular ideas, which must already exist in the public sphere, are the ones that are promoted. New ideas are risky and don't guarantee sales, so profit-driven institutions don't support them and thus don't promote creativity; the ideas they publish are just recycled ones in new formats.

Also, the education system promotes conformity and not creativity. If you want a degree from a university, then you have to accept what that degree course preaches. You cannot challenge or oppose the ideology of that course; if you do, you won't graduate! So just like a soldier having to follow orders to remain a soldier, students have to answer questions in the way they are told to in order to pass and graduate. And if you don't pass and graduate, the threat of unemployment, financial difficulty, and social exclusion looms—a good incentive to conform, it would seem. Additionally, the education system promotes a specific paradigm. For instance, you can get a degree in evolutionary biology, but you cannot get a degree in a model offering an alternative view on the causation of biodiversity (such as Lamarckism, mutationism, or orthogenesis). Thus the paradigm is set-up to reinforce itself and eliminate opposing paradigms.

But people outside the institution are not constrained by it, and are, therefore, in a better position to exercise free-thinking and consequently challenge the institution's ideas. This is possibly why many major scientific breakthroughs and revolutions come from people working outside the institution. For instance, Albert Einstein was working as a patent clerk when he revolutionised physics with his theory of relativity. Although, of course, the institution determines which ideas can be entertained and presented. Einstein's ideas were welcomed because they fit into the general paradigm; ideas that don't fit, such as those that imply non-natural phenomena, are likely to be disregarded.

Small changes within the academic establishment are possible, such as tweaking certain theories, but major ideological shifts, such as going from materialism to spiritual philosophy, are nigh impossible to bring about, because consensuses, just like people in general, are resistant to change.[13] Understandably... Why change a good thing? The status quo clearly serves the people "at the top", thus there is no incentive for them to change it. And, as they are the ones who control the flow of information, shifting the paradigm without their support is a challenging task. So if you don't appeal to an already existing market, or you don't conform with the main educational institutions, how do you get your ideas in front of the masses? Well, it seems you can't (unless the system makes an exception).

Many academics press the importance of "peer-review" and have become heavily reliant on it.[14] But peer-review has significant limitations.[15] At times, it seems that personal experience should trump what you are told. Consider this example: if you are a doctor and the peer-reviewed literature states that *Treatment A* irrefutably cures *Illness B*, then you are obligated to prescribe *Treatment A* for *Illness B*. However, if you notice in your practice that this treatment has no effect on *Illness B* in your patients, then your personal experience may give rise to scepticism over the peer-reviewed consensus, as there are conflicting conclusions.

---

13 Materialism (or physicalism) is a metaphysical philosophy that asserts that matter is the fundamental substance in nature, meaning everything can be reduced to physical matter and explained by physical (natural) processes. Thus materialism claims that the mind is an emergent property of the body/brain. Materialism and physicalism are, broadly speaking, synonymous with naturalism.

14 Peer-reviewing is the process of having scholarly work, ideas, or research submitted for the scrutiny of those considered "experts" in the field.

15 Peer-review is highly valued in contemporary academia, but there is no law to say that having work peer-reviewed (or championed by other people) makes it more credible. Also, the peer-review process is controlled by institutions that promote fixed ways of thinking, thus limiting creativity and opposing new ideas or paradigm shifts.

So let's say you have 100 patients with *Illness B* and observe that none of them respond to *Treatment A*, then the question arises: Am I going to believe the peer-reviewed consensus or believe my personal experience? You may stick with the consensus by doubting or denying your own experience (informational influence): you could claim you are hallucinating or perceiving an illusion, or you could appeal to a probability argument, such as that proposed by Guildenstern when Rosencrantz flips coins and gets ninety-two heads in a row in Tom Stoppard's 1966 play *Rosencrantz and Guildenstern Are Dead*; or you could make other excuses, like the tests are inaccurate or the patients are lying.[16] Or perhaps you may be drawn into the consensus due to normative influence, such as conformity, loyalty, self-preservation, remaining part of a group, lower risk in being wrong (the error is shouldered by the group rather than you as an individual), maintaining position in society, and so on. It is for these reasons that many people opt for the consensus over personal experience in such instances.

But some people would back their personal experience and claim that something odd is going on. And personal experience should not be considered weaker than the consensus as a source of "knowledge". If you perceived a ghost, presumably you wouldn't resort to the consensus of "ghosts don't exist" to doubt your own experience. So similarly, if someone tells you that they perceived a ghost, it seems unreasonable to resort to the consensus of "ghosts don't exist" to dismiss *their* claim.

---

16 Guildenstern witnesses Rosencrantz flip 96 heads in a row during a betting game, but there is no cheating (the coins are not weighted or double-headed). This initially leads Guildenstern to postulate mystical or supernatural explanations, but he eventually concludes that there is no mystery and thus no special explanation is required, as "each individual coin spun individually is as likely to come down heads as tails and therefore should cause no surprise each time it does". A mathematical theory known as *Ranking Theory*, proposed by contemporary German philosopher Wolfgang Spohn, can be used to justify this claim.

Such a notion, however, would have huge implications for the discipline of psychiatry, which is based on the premise that individual experiences and beliefs that are unusual, or at odds with the majority, are unrepresentative of reality and thus pathological. So if ten people are in a room and one of them perceives a ghost while the other nine do not, then the one is considered wrong. But there is no fundamental law to support this view; instead, the nine could be wrong.

## *Psychological Bias – Internal Factors*

Recent studies in neuroscience and psychology have established that people typically rationalise evidence in a way that fits what they want to believe, and what's more, actively seek evidence that will support their beliefs.[17, 18] And science is not exempt from this phenomenon. Many scientists have a bias towards science and the scientific process; they have a tendency to see things that appeal to their scientific perspective and seek these out. Also, a scientist who bases his career on a "scientific" claim, needs it to be true, so he is more likely to see the evidence *for* it than the evidence *against* it. It is a simple case of self-preservation and is not necessarily intentional. He *needs* it to be true in order to sustain his position in society. This also dictates how he interprets information as evidence.

Helen Longino, an American philosopher of science, proposes that an individual's assumptions about the relationship between

---

[17] Paula Kaanders, Pradyumna Sepulveda, Tomas Folke, Pietro Ortoleva and Benedetto De Martino, "Humans actively sample evidence to support prior beliefs," *eLife* 11 (April 2022): e71768. doi: 10.7554/eLife.71768

[18] Filip Gesiarz, Donal Cahill and Tali Sharot, "Evidence accumulation is biased by motivation: A computational account," *PLOS Computational Biology* 15, no. 6 (June 2019): e1007089. doi: 10.1371/journal.pcbi.1007089

observations and a hypothesis will determine whether that individual considers the observations as evidence for the hypothesis.[19] So information (data and observations) can be interpreted in different ways to create evidence for a particular hypothesis. Even though the information itself is objective, the lens through which it is viewed determines the way in which it is interpreted.

An excellent example to demonstrate this is the case of Charles Darwin and his formulation of the theory of evolution by natural selection. The idea of common descent and evolution had already been proposed by his grandfather, Erasmus Darwin, in his 1794 book *Zoonomia*, and Charles Darwin reportedly, and unsurprisingly, was influenced by his grandfather's idea. So Charles Darwin clearly had the evolution explanation in mind *before* he undertook any specific investigation of nature. Consequently, he set out to try and prove his preconceived explanation. And, of course, he would have had a bias for his own explanation (partly because that was his path to stardom), resulting in a motivation to prove his explanation right rather than establish the truth. This bias is likely to have influenced his interpretation of the data and observations. And the data and observations he used to support his theory could easily be, and in fact *were* by the majority of antecedent leading naturalists, interpreted in a completely different way.

Consider the person who believes in aliens. They could consider crop circles as evidence for aliens, but without belief in aliens, it would be impossible to conclude that aliens were responsible; those without a belief in aliens, or without the concept of aliens, are more likely to see the crop circles as evidence of human pranks. Similarly, Darwin's preconceived belief that evolution was true, led him to see evolution in nature, while

---

[19] Helen Longino, "Evidence and Hypothesis: An Analysis of Evidential Relations," *Philosophy of Science* 46 (1979): 35-56.

naturalists without an awareness or belief in evolution did not see evolution in nature. In this manner, the same information can be used to support conflicting hypotheses (or spun into "evidence" for opposing claims).

Evidence emerges when raw data and observations are used to support a specific claim. Thus evidence requires an interpreter and an interpretation process, and these make it subjective and vulnerable to psychological bias. This also leads some to argue that, as all science requires an observer to interpret the data and observations, there is no such thing as value-free science. Not so long ago, the scientific community championed "white intellectual superiority" and used "evidence", such as cranial capacity data, archaeology, and intelligence studies, to support it. The raw data and observations that led to this "evidence" would not be interpreted today in the way it was then. And it's not inconceivable that, a few decades from now, future generations will look back and ridicule current scientific theories (perhaps evolutionary theory or the germ theory of disease), similar to the way most educated people today look back and ridicule race science.

The same issue applies to statistics and "studies". These can be cherry-picked and presented in variable ways to support preconceived claims. Consider this: in January 2021, referring to the global pandemic of the Covid-19 virus, the prominent newspaper *USA Today* headlined a statistic to show the death count of Americans dying from Covid-19 had surpassed the death count of Americans who died in World War II.[20] The use of this statistic was (presumably) intended to cause shock, but it is extremely

---

20 Jim Sergent and Ramon Padilla, "Americans dying faster of Covid-19 than our soldiers did in WWII," *USA Today* (January 19, 2021): Para. 1. https://eu.usatoday.com/in-depth/news/2021/01/19/covid-19-deaths-americans-dying-faster-than-our-soldiers-did-wwii/6602717002/

misleading, as it does not tell the whole story. For instance, it doesn't reveal that over 80% of American deaths from Covid-19 were in people over the age of 65, nor that over 90% of those who died had at least one pre-existing medical condition, while, of course, the vast majority of American deaths in World War II were soldiers (typically young, fit men). So the average American who died in World War II would have been expected to have had perhaps another fifty years of life had the war not happened, whereas the average American who died from Covid-19 would have been expected to have had perhaps another five years of life had the Covid-19 outbreak not occurred. Thus comparing the two groups is unreasonable. Even though the statistic is true, it was used in a misleading manner to give the false impression that the Covid-19 pandemic was more devastating than World War II. Such play with statistics is typically done in politics to inflame passions. These passions can then dictate how future information is interpreted.

Bias is obviously present in all walks of life. In 1994, O.J. Simpson, a famous black American sportsman, was accused of murdering his white American wife Nicole Brown Simpson and her friend Ron Goldman. The trial was described as one of the most publicised criminal trials in human history, and was portrayed extensively in the American media. Following the verdict, an NBC News poll in 1995 revealed that 75% of white people thought that O.J. Simpson was guilty, whereas 70% of black people thought that he was innocent.[21] A subsequent NBC poll taken in 2004 returned similar results, with 87% of white people thinking Simpson was guilty, and 70% of black people thinking he

---

21 CNN-Time Magazine Poll, "Races disagree on impact of Simpson Trial," *CNN*, October 6, 1995. www.edition.cnn.com/US/OJ/daily/9510/10-06/poll_race/oj_pol_txt.html.

was innocent.²² (These statistics seem reasonable to use for the point about to be made.) If we presume that in each poll, the two groups had access to the same evidence and had similar levels of intelligence, then the most reasonable conclusion to draw is that the vast difference in judgement was due to underlying bias. This is a great example to demonstrate that knowledge claims are not based on empirical evidence or reason but rather on intuition or underlying psychological factors—bias, not evidence, leads to one's beliefs.

Politics, religion, and sport are classic examples of bias. Take opposing coaches watching their sides during a football match... During the match, an incident is often interpreted in opposing ways by the two coaches. What appears to one coach to be a foul *on* a player is seen by the other as simulation (feigning injury) *by* the player. But, of course, they are witnessing the same event. It is all a matter of interpretation. The coaches are more likely to see the event in the way they are expected to see it by their peers and in a way that favours their own outlook and desired outcome.

Most people in the world are born into one of the major religions. And most people in the world adopt the religion they were born into as the religion they choose to follow and believe in. It forms part of their identity. The result is different people of equal intelligence living, believing in, and following completely different religious doctrines. Equally intelligent people of different religions argue the case for their own religion because of their bias towards it. They genuinely believe that their way is correct. It is not that they are trying to deliberately mislead or deceive; they are just blind to

---

22 Jennifer De Pinto, Fred Backus, Kabir Khanna and Anthony Salvanto, "Poll: only 27 percent of Americans think O.J. Simpson will regain celebrity status," *CBS News*, September 29, 2017. https://www.cbsnews.com/news/o-j-simpson-poll-celebrity-status/.

arguments that go against their religious ideology. (This is the same way that political and sociological ideologies work.)

Contentious and hotly debated issues in the world, such as socialism-versus-capitalism, euthanasia, and capital punishment, can be argued well from both sides of the debate. Proponents of such views often interpret new observations and statistics in a way that supports their preconceived position, and are resistant to information that challenges their position. This phenomenon is supported by research from modern neuroscience and psychology which shows that it is astonishingly difficult to change a person's mind about anything.

But it is not just the interpretation of the observations that is subject to bias. The observations themselves are based in psychological conditioning. Perception is subjective. For instance, using my earlier example, if you are heavily convinced by the success of *Treatment A* for *Illness B*, then you may start seeing the success of the treatment even if it is not there. (Obviously, disciplines that lack objective physical tests, like psychiatry, are more prone to this.)

Apophenia is the phenomenon of perceiving meaningful patterns or connections in random or meaningless observations. It describes the tendency of human beings to seek patterns in random information and has been typically used as an explanation to discredit religious experiences of people. But it can be equally used to explain how scientists see patterns or causes that fulfil expectations or substantiate preconceived ideas.

Typically, an author will read his manuscript several times in an attempt to eradicate all the mistakes contained within it. Eventually, he will be satisfied that the book reads fine and there are no typos or errors in punctuation or grammar. However, errors undoubtedly would have made their way into his book. Many of these errors would ordinarily be picked up by the author if he was reading them with a fresh mind for the first time, or if he was reading them in someone else's work. The reason that he misses his own errors is because, after a while, the mind starts interpreting its perceptual experiences in a way that fits in with the desired and expected outcome. He reads what he is *expecting* to read rather than what he is *actually* reading. His mind automatically corrects errors and fills in gaps. This is the inevitable process of mental conditioning—a point comes where the mind is no longer able to see errors nor evaluate accurately.

A pertinent example of this is the McGurk Effect, which is a phenomenon whereby the mind interprets perceptions incorrectly based on previous conditioning... Psychological experiments have shown that people struggle to identify the correct substance of a drink when the colour of that drink is changed. If strawberry juice is changed in colour to gold (resembling apple juice), people report tasting apple juice when drinking the golden strawberry juice.[23] They *think* that they are drinking apple juice, but the reality is that they aren't. There is a misinterpretation of the perceptual experience due to an underlying bias caused by mental conditioning. So essentially, the more conditioned you become, the more incapable you are of fairly and indiscriminately evaluating information which contradicts what you want and expect to be correct.

Also, the mind is only able to perceive that which it has a preconceived notion of. But, you might ask, doesn't this lead to a regress problem because all preconceived notions have to start from somewhere? Well, this is the mysterious process of mental conditioning where perceptual ability is gradually built up through living and experience. It is not clear what a baby perceives: they may not be having the same subjective experience (qualia) as you are, despite being exposed to the same external stimulus—their eyes may be

---

[23] BBC Horizon, "Is Seeing Believing," *BBC*, Ep. 4 (2010–11): 23:00. https://www.bbc.co.uk/programmes/b00vhw1d.

directed towards the same object as yours, but they may not be seeing that object in the same way as you are.

This idea is demonstrated with the "ships not seen" anecdote(s) from European exploration to the Americas and Australia... It is claimed that when some of the first European explorers arrived by ships to these lands, the indigenous peoples on the coastlines showed no response: it seemed that the native people could not see the ships even though they were only a few dozen metres away and clearly visible. It is suggested that this was because the ships were alien to their experience (i.e. they did not have a preconceived notion of a ship) and thus their visual perception could not instantly register the new experience. A similar phenomenon has been noted in some cultures that live in dense forests and seem to lack a notion of distance: when they are taken to an open field for the first time and see a cow in the distance, they consider the cow to be really small rather than being far away.[24]

Another example used to highlight the limitations of perception is the "rabbit-duck illusion", as shown below:

---

24 Colin Turnbull, *The Forest People*. (London: Franklin Classics, 2018), 251–253.

The picture is an ambiguous one in that either a rabbit or duck can be seen. It was used in 1899 by Joseph Jastrow (an American psychologist) to demonstrate that perception is not just what one sees but also a mental activity. Ludwig Wittgenstein (an Austrian-British philosopher and one of the most influential philosophers of the 20th Century) used it a few decades later to describe two different ways of seeing (a phenomenon known as *aspect perception*). Whether a person sees a rabbit or duck when looking at the picture is based on various factors, but firstly, the person can only see either the rabbit or the duck if they have a notion of them. For instance, if a person is familiar with rabbits but unfamiliar with ducks (i.e. they have never come across a duck before), then they will see the rabbit and not the duck. And vice versa. And if a person has no notion of either a rabbit or duck, then they will see just a bunch of meaningless squiggles; such may be the case with members of lost tribes in jungles or rainforests who have never come across either of these animals.[25] This same principle could apply to not just a picture but a real phenomenon too, and this would account for the "ships not seen" phenomenon. Thus what you perceive, and *if* you perceive, are based on some prior underlying mental conditioning.

Another view proposes that your mind creates perceptual experiences independent of external objects or stimuli—the phenomena you perceive are actually constructs of your mind and based on underlying mental causes. This is known as idealism

---

25 Note, in a sense, or from one perspective, the picture *is* just a bunch of meaningless squiggles, and therefore a person who views it as such cannot be said to be wrong: there is no correct way to view the picture (unless one appeals to the intent of the illustrator); it can be viewed as a rabbit, a duck, or a bunch of meaningless squiggles. However, the same cannot be said about a real phenomenon: for instance, if you perceive a snake to be a rope, then it *can* be said that you are perceiving the phenomenon incorrectly.

(explained later) and is analogous to how a dream is a creation and projection of your mind—you have perceptual experiences (or perception-like experiences) when dreaming but these are not related to true or independent external phenomena. So perhaps your desires lead to your perceptions. For instance, if you desire a particular result from an experiment, then perhaps your will can induce the experience of perceiving this result. In such a case, the perception is not false, but it has been caused by the mind and thus does not reflect or represent an objective reality.

In summary, all your ideologies, belief systems, philosophical worldviews, and knowledge claims are based on psychological factors (bias) and not on evidence or reason; evidence and reason are just used as means to justify these after the fact. However, it's a common misconception to think that bias is inevitable and necessary. It can be removed, as demonstrated by Socrates when he claimed to know nothing, and Descartes when he produced the *Cogito*: they both stripped all the psychological biases from their psyches yet were still able to live, function, and have meaningful interactions with the world.

Hence you can accept certain claims for practical functioning without subscribing strongly or irreversibly to any idea. And contrary to what you might think, this position is liberating, not confining, as you are free of meaningless ideologies that restrict you and dictate your experiences. The process of detaching yourself from existing ideologies is known as mental deconditioning or "emptying thyself".

## *Theism Versus Atheism*

Of course, in order to live and function in the world, we have to assume truths, such as assuming that our sense faculties are reliable. And in order to engage in any rational discourse, we typically accept the fundamental laws of logic. If we did not, we could not formulate any ideas and would be stuck in Descartes' *Cogito*. So we can make meaningful determinations if we agree on the unjustified starting axioms. But of questions of the fundamental nature of reality, starting axioms are not universally agreed upon, and consequently there is much debate and argument over such questions.

For instance, a theist typically asserts that there must be a non-natural or intelligent cause for the material universe. Whereas, the naturalist (or materialist) works on the starting assumption that all phenomena are reducible to physical matter and naturalistic causes. Thus there is no agreement on the starting axioms here and neither party can be said to be right or wrong.

This is why debate between theists and non-theists on the existence of God becomes a meaningless affair. Neither party can prove their position or disprove the other. It is a waste of everybody's time and is like two boys arguing that their own mother's cooking is better than the other's.

So the question of whether God exists is not one that is addressed using reason or empirical means. It is based on one's psychological disposition and whether they "want" to believe or not, i.e. their faith. But, often, theists try to justify their faith-based position after the fact, using reason or empiricism. It's cart-before-the-horse stuff. All knowledge is. Theistic belief, like any other belief, is built on unjustified axioms (presuppositions) that are based on some kind of intuition.

Therefore, theists who claim that they believe in God based on (objective) evidence, are kidding themselves. So too are non-theists who claim that they reject God based on evidence (or a lack thereof). The truth is that they intuitively believe or don't believe and then look for the evidence to support and substantiate their preconceived position. (Note, some believers may believe not because of intuition but because of some socio-cultural factors, such as conforming with family and friends, but this should not be considered true belief, as there is no internal resonation with the message—the person is simply pretending.)

When it comes to the question of God, there are three possibilities: theism, atheism, or agnosticism (undecided). Some atheists like to claim that atheism includes agnosticism, as atheism just refers to lacking theism, so it is both the undecided position as well as the positive claim that theism is untrue. But this muddies the water. There needs to be a means by which the positive claim can be distinguished from the undecided position. Granted, they do this by creating two sub-categories of atheism: positive atheism (the active claim that theism is false) and negative atheism (agnosticism). But this is inadequate, as there is a significant distinction between these two positions, meaning they should not be classified under the umbrella term of "atheism".

To highlight why, consider materialism. Typically, a positive atheist is a materialist and a theist is a non-materialist (or an amaterialist). But for a theist to argue that people who are genuinely undecided about the fundamental nature of reality should also be known as amaterialists, would be an unreasonable request—the theist would be inappropriately collecting agnostics on this issue into his category (a category that supports the claim that materialism is wrong). So for any claim, there should be three categories or positions you can hold: affirmation, negation, or undecided. To bracket the negation and undecided positions together is an error.

Materialists typically argue that scientific knowledge is superior to non-scientific empirical knowledge (knowledge acquired through experience without using the scientific method). Consequently, if an individual has a one-time personal experience that leads them to theism, then this is dismissed as an inappropriate source of knowledge, as the experience is not conducive to the scientific method (it is not testable or repeatable). However, as we've previously intimated, there are a couple of reasons to suggest that scientific knowledge is not necessarily superior to non-scientific empirical knowledge...

Consider knowledge of how an apple tastes. You can acquire this by eating one apple, ten apples, one hundred apples, or one thousand apples. The point at which you determine when "knowledge" of how apples taste arises seems subjective and arbitrary. There is a case to say that eating one apple can give you as much knowledge on this topic as eating one hundred apples can. And this refers to Hume's problem of induction. Remember, Rosencrantz flipped ninety-two heads in a row, so what's to say that you haven't, by chance, stumbled upon one hundred stale apples in a row and been misled into thinking apples taste foul when, in fact, they do not? We can use the black swan fallacy to highlight this point: if you test one hundred swans and observe that they are all white, then your knowledge cannot be considered superior to that of the person who tests two swans and observes that one is white and one is black. Also, as demonstrated with the McGurk effect, previous experience conditions future experience and therefore can result in a self-fulfilling prophecy phenomenon. So psychologically, if you expect apples to taste the same as previous ones, then this expectation affects the taste experience of future apples, thus rendering repeatability futile—one hundred apples tasting a certain way is not necessarily more informative than one apple tasting that same way. The point being, if a person claims a one-time personal experience, such as a "vision", that leads them to theism, then this should not be regarded as non-knowledge just because it is not repeatable or testable.

Another error is to make the distinction where theism refers to belief (and thus atheism a lack of belief) and gnosis refers to knowledge (and thus agnosticism a lack of knowledge). Separating knowledge from belief in epistemology is a contentious venture, as all knowledge claims are technically beliefs (as argued earlier). Thus it becomes an arbitrary issue—what one person considers belief, another may consider knowledge. In fact, to claim that you are an "agnostic theist", as some people do, is somewhat of a contradiction in terms. Because, the notion that "I do not know for sure, but I strongly believe" is the underpinning of all knowledge claims, and therefore to emphasise this for theistic belief is meaningless, as theistic beliefs are no different from non-theistic beliefs. And clearly, there is no need to add the word "agnostic" in front of every ideology you subscribe to. For instance, you wouldn't say "I'm an agnostic evolutionist" or "I'm an agnostic capitalist" or "I'm an agnostic helio-centrist", because the uncertainty is simply inferred. So it is more apt to consider agnosticism the genuinely undecided position and atheism the *active* negation of theism.

But the New Atheist movement has recently tried to shift attitudes and change the definition of atheism to include agnosticism so that there are only two groups instead of three. They may do this for socio-political and census reasons: having agnostics identify as atheists inflates their numbers, and consequently the appeal of atheism. Most advocates of atheism and members of the New Atheist movement, however, are positive atheists and not agnostics; they make the active knowledge claim that God does not exist and thus have a burden of proof. So the irony is, positive atheism is a belief system that requires just as much faith as theism.

And it can be argued that positive atheists do not just make a claim that something (God) does not exist, but also a claim that something does exist. Because, if you accept that the fundamental essence of reality is either material (not God) or non-material (God), then to actively reject God is to not only make the claim that *the fundamental essence of reality is not non-material*, but to also make the claim that *the fundamental essence of reality is material*.

(God, defined here, is the non-natural substratum and fundamental essence of everything. Now, it can be argued that there are only two potential fundamental substances: mental stuff [non-material] and physical stuff [material]. Or mind and matter. So to claim that the fundamental substance or essence is non-material is to claim that it is mental, i.e. a mind or intelligence. And thus God also becomes the non-material *intelligent* cause of everything.)

An atheist rejects God by claiming that there is no evidence for it. But there is no evidence against it either! And there never can be direct empirical evidence for or against it, because, by definition, it is a non-natural (non-material) entity and consequently cannot be investigated through physical means. Therefore, it can only be known, if at all, through non-perceptual means.

# PART 2 –
# THE SOLUTION BY SPIRITUAL PHILOSOPHY

## *The Beginning of Spirituality*

Descartes' *Cogito* is a conclusion derived from intuition, not sense experience or reason—you intuit that you exist, you don't perceive it or reason it.[26] So the only truth you can *know* with your human mind comes from intuition. And this is the beginning point of spirituality: the realisation that I exist and this is the only thing I know; everything else could be an illusion. Then the internal spiritual enquiry into "Who am I?" begins. Who is the thinker of these thoughts? Who is the perceiver of these perceptions? Who is the feeler of these feelings? Spiritual philosophy,

---

[26] There are some philosophers who argue that the *Cogito* is derived from reason wherein the conclusion "I am" is deduced from the premise "I think". Descartes himself offered the following response to such a view: *"And when someone says I am thinking, therefore I am, or exist, he is not deducing existence from thought by means of a syllogism, but recognises it as known directly by a simple intuition of the mind."* (Charles Adam and Paul Tannery, eds., *Oeuvres de Descartes*. [Paris: Leopold Cerf., 1904], VII 140.) Regardless of whether the *Cogito* is considered intuitive or deductive, spiritual philosophy claims that "I exist" is a self-evident sensation and thus must be based in intuition, not reason: one does not go from the realisation that "I think" to the conclusion that "I exist" but rather just automatically knows that "I exist"—it is not the fact that one is thinking that leads them to realise they exist, but that the very presence of conscious experience (e.g. thinking) *is* the state of knowing "I exist". That is, "I think" (my thinking) is an extension of "I exist" (my existence) and thus they are not separate facts that can be connected by way of a syllogism—"I exist" is implicit in the premise "I think", as to think, one must exist. Thus, metaphysically speaking (or from reality's point of view or God's perspective), it is actually, "I exist, therefore I think."

via the spiritual scriptures and spiritual teachers, reveals these answers to you. (Descartes, instead of going inwards into the self and addressing these fundamental spiritual questions, opted to go back outwards into the world to answer further questions on the lower knowledge of the external world.)

The reality is God (this will be expounded later). Spiritual philosophy deals with information pertaining to the reality. And according to spiritual philosophy, the reality is imperceptible and inconceivable—the sense faculties and the rational capacities of the human mind are simply incapable of discerning it. Therefore, information about it transcends conventional human capability. This was claimed by Immanuel Kant when he said the noumenon (the metaphysical reality underpinning the phenomenal universe and phenomenal experience) can never be known. But spiritual philosophy disagrees here; it says it *can* be known...

By asking the following question, the Chandogya Upanishad (a Hindu scripture) indirectly affirms that knowledge of the reality can be obtained: *"Have you acquired that knowledge by which the unknown is known?"* (Chandogya Upanishad 6:1:3). The very question implies that there is a means by which "the unknown" (the reality) can be known. And according to spiritual philosophy, it is known through salvation.

But in order to attain knowledge of the reality, information about it (separate from knowledge) has to be given (revealed) to you—this is the only way you can learn of it. And this information, which is propounded by spiritual philosophy, is claimed to have been directly *revealed* from a higher source (Divine revelation). So information about the reality comes from *outside* a person.

The basis for spiritual philosophy is that there *is* a cosmic creator who has created you and the external world with a purpose, and He reveals this purpose to humanity, and you, accordingly. The ultimate purpose is to *know* the reality. The scriptures, messiahs, and saints reveal the *way* to knowledge (or experience) of the reality. And this knowledge is obtained through non-mental, non-perceptual experience, not through the mind via either intellectual determination or perception. It is a state of existence. So you can experience it, and this experience gives you full knowledge of it.

As reason comes from *within* the person, the claim that reason reflects the reality is an unprovable and arbitrary assertion—it is a faith, but one that can never be confirmed. So if you are a naturalist and start with the premise (faith) that sense experience and reason are the only tools for gaining knowledge of the reality, then you can *never know* the reality, because the possibility of all beliefs being erroneous can never be excluded. But if you start with faith in spiritual philosophy's assertion that there is a cosmic creator who can lead you to knowledge of the reality, then you *can know* the reality.

As stated earlier, all beliefs (knowledge claims) have to start with faith, and spiritual philosophy is no different; acceptance of spiritual philosophy starts with faith, and this faith is a prerequisite for knowledge of the reality. But note, spiritual philosophy is not in itself evidence of God; you start with faith in God and then use spiritual philosophy to *know* God. And faith in God starts with humility. You must accept that your intellect on its own is useless at discerning the reality. Thus humility is integral to acquiring knowledge of the reality, and this is why, in the Christian tradition, pride is considered the deadliest of the seven deadly sins.

So the starting point of spiritual philosophy, and subsequently the spiritual path, is the realisation that you cannot build up (or deduce) information about the reality, or acquire knowledge of the reality, by yourself. As Western philosophy tends to value reason and perceptual experience over revelation, many academics, in particular the logical empiricists, have a hard time accepting this. They want to work out this information themselves using their own (limited) abilities, though doing so is like looking in a dark room for a black cat that isn't *in* the room—to continue looking in the room for the cat on the notion that eventually it will be found is clearly an error. Hence the logical empiricist goes as far as he can on his quest for knowledge, but eventually he hits a wall, on the other side of which lies the reality, and neither his rationalism nor his empiricism can break through the wall to access the reality. That's where spiritual philosophy reaches out and says: "I can take you to the reality provided you replace your faith in rationalism and empiricism with faith in revelation."[27]

Spiritual philosophy urges you to drop all your current beliefs, as these limit you. You may ask, how is a person supposed to function if they cannot believe in anything? Well, there is a difference between belief and acceptance: the degree of conviction. A belief is a strong conviction that is resistant to removal. Mere acceptance, on the other hand, is amenable to removal or change because it has no underlying motivating factor.

Religion is a typical example of a belief rather than an acceptance. A religionist holds on to his particular religious doctrine and will not let it go. But, similarly, many scientific claims, especially those related to the fundamental existential questions, such as the origin of consciousness, the origin of the cosmos, and the origin

---

[27] Cf. the penultimate proposition in Ludwig's Wittgenstein's book *Tractatus Logico-Philosophicus* (1921): *"My propositions serve as elucidations in the following way: anyone who understands me recognises them as nonsensical, when he has used them – as steps – to climb beyond them. (He must, so to speak, throw away the ladder after he has climbed up it.) He must transcend these propositions, and then he will see the world aright."* Interestingly, Wittgenstein, in a certain later note (1930), returns to his ladder metaphor as follows: *"I might say: if the place I want to get to could only be reached by way of a ladder, I would give up trying to get there. For the place I really have to get to is a place I must already be at now. Anything that I might reach by climbing a ladder does not interest me."*

of species, are beliefs rather than acceptances. Many scientists, and followers of science, dogmatically conserve their naturalistic answers to such questions and are resistant to having them challenged, although granted, they may accept having them tweaked slightly. (There is a disingenuity in such a scientist's position, as he claims he follows the evidence and can [and will] change his mind if led to, but he *can't*, as all his ideas are founded on the unprovable axiom of materialism.)

The instruction is to not believe but instead *accept* ideas and claims for practical purposes and functioning. For instance, you don't have to believe that climate change is true, but you can accept it based on the scientific consensus and thus adapt your life accordingly, such as recycling and being more efficient with your energy use; these changes are not particularly troublesome or life-changing, so even if climate change is false, you do not lose much in making such changes. (Though, a problem arises if you think that the changes harm you, like some people think with certain interventions, such as vaccinations or policing.) The importance of this no-doctrine mind state, where you are free of all ideologies and worldviews, is highlighted in the Bhagavad Gita: "*Just as fire is enveloped by smoke, as a mirror by dust, and as an embryo by amnion, so also by that this is covered*" (Bhagavad Gita 3:38).[28]

Swami Yogeshwarananda, a mystic of the ancient Advaita Vedanta order of India, explains the meaning of this verse. He says that the layer of dust on the mirror represents the psychological baggage, including all the strong ideologies you subscribe to, that prevents you from seeing the reality. (The other two analogies in this verse [the enveloping of fire by smoke and the covering of the embryo by the amniotic sac] refer to other spiritual truths.)

---

28 Translation by Swami Yogeshwarananda.

To further elucidate this idea, Swami Yogeshwarananda also gives the analogy of how one has to clear the debris on the surface of a pond before they can see the bottom of the pond.

This teaching is also given by Jesus in two parables. Before we mention them, it's important to note that the parables used by Jesus are mystical in content and require spiritual wisdom for interpretation and understanding. Jesus himself implies this: when asked by his disciples why he uses parables when speaking to the crowds, he responded by saying, *"Because the knowledge of the secrets of the Kingdom of Heaven has been given to you, but not to them"* (Matt 13:11 [NIV]). Swami Yogeshwarananda provides the mystical explanations of the parables of Jesus.

In one parable, Jesus says, *"Neither do people pour new wine into old wineskins. If they do, the skins will burst; the wine will run out and the wineskins will be ruined. No, they pour new wine into new wineskins, and both are preserved"* (Matt 9:17). In another parable, a king puts on a grand wedding feast and invites many people, but one person attends in old clothes not fitting for the occasion, so the king throws him out of the feast.

Swami Yogeshwarananda says that these parables are used to demonstrate the importance of mental deconditioning. New wine, representing the new spiritual teachings, can only enter a person who is open-minded (has a new, fresh mind that is not full of old teachings and old ideologies). Similarly, the wedding feast parable represents the idea of wearing new clothes in order to partake in the glorious feast of spiritual knowledge that Jesus is offering. If you listen to such teachings with an old attitude, old ideologies, and old doctrines (old clothes), then you are not fit to listen to them and will not be able to understand the teachings (partake in the wedding feast). And the first step of the spiritual path is the hearing of the spiritual teachings. This is known as *sravana* in Hindu thought.

Then there is a second meaning to these parables, which is the idea that one should empty themselves *completely* and free themselves of all mental attachments, beliefs, ideas (including the teachings of spiritual philosophy), and even all mental activity, in order to attain salvation. This is the last step of the spiritual path.

So initially, you clear yourself of all old ideas, and then the new spiritual ideas enter you. And these are just like a finger pointing out the moon; they eventually lead you to experience the moon, which you can only do once you stop looking at the finger and instead look to where the finger is pointing. The final step is to drop even the faith that precipitated the whole process.

As said, spiritual philosophy implores you to not subscribe to any ideology, whether it be scientific or religious. (Spiritual philosophy is opposed to institutional religion.) But then you may ask, what about the ideology of spiritual philosophy? Well, this is just the means used to get you out of indoctrination, like the finger pointing at the moon; once the moon has been discerned, the finger has served its purpose and is no longer of any use, and can be discarded. That's why the final teaching of spiritual philosophy pronounces, *now forget all this teaching*.

Thus there is an important distinction to be made: The spiritual teachings simply provide *information about* the reality; they do not give *knowledge of* the reality. This is analogous to how the finger pointing out the moon does not give you knowledge or experience of the moon; it simply *leads* you to knowledge and experience of the moon.

Note, "knowledge of the reality" is synonymous with "experience of the reality". However, this experience is non-perceptual and non-mental, as revealed by the Upanishads via the following statement about the reality: "*The senses cannot perceive it nor the mind conceive it*" (Katha Upanishad 2:3:12). And this experience is referred to by various terms, including: *nirvana*, enlightenment, salvation, liberation, *moksha,* God-experience, and Self-realisation.

The objective is to remain sceptical and agnostic on all worldly matters. Some empiricists claim that this is what they do through fallibilism, whereby they accept that there are no certain truths. But this is typically a semantic error. Their approach is still one of belief and not mere acceptance or agnosticism. This is inferred by the passion they demonstrate in defending their position. As soon as you identify with one position over another, you have demonstrated belief and not agnosticism, even if you claim that your belief is open to change with new "evidence". A truly wise person, at least according to Socrates, would not lean towards any doctrine.

Spiritual philosophy is a doctrine of no doctrine and thus is not really a doctrine. Some people may argue that this is actually a type of doctrine, but it isn't, in the same way that no food is not a type of cuisine. A doctrine should be self-fulfilling, whereas the doctrine of spiritual philosophy is self-defeating because it leads to its own destruction by promoting a state of no doctrine. But spiritual philosophy does have to provide a semi-doctrine to promote the no-doctrine state. The actual doctrine of spiritual philosophy is pure silence. This is because, as Ludwig Wittgenstein claimed, the most important things cannot be talked about, as language is limited; language describes, but that which matters most is indescribable, and therefore is best represented through silence.

This is presumably why when Yogaswami, a saint of Jaffna, met Sri Ramana Maharishi, a saint of Tamil Nadu, they remained in pure silence, staring at each other, and then, after some time, parted company without having said a single word. The encounter was provided as a profound teaching to others. Of course, non-silent teachings must also be given; non-silence must be used to promote silence, as the teacher can only convey the importance of silence by using non-silence. But the non-silence is just the means.

## *The Criteria for Spirituality*

The spiritual path is a science. It is testable. Self-testable, that is. If you follow the instructions, you will gain knowledge of the reality. And once you know the reality, you *know* the reality. There is no doubt. It is said to be complete and unwavering knowledge. The seers/experiencers of this (the saints) testify to it. And the scriptures affirm it. Of course, you have to have faith in them and the process, but *if* they are true, then knowledge of the reality *can* be obtained. This is the only means by which it can be.

Faith in the scriptures, the teachers, and the process, is the forerunner of knowledge of the reality. Without this faith, you cannot and will not engage in the process of knowing the reality, and thereby will remain ignorant of it.

But where does this faith come from and how can one develop it? It comes from being good. This enables an internal psychological resonation with the spiritual teaching, which results in *faith* in the spiritual teaching. The message of spiritual philosophy is not overly complex. You do not require a high degree of intelligence to comprehend it, but you do need a good nature in order to resonate with it and thus understand it—only a good person can understand and resonate with the spiritual teachings. This constitutes the science of spirituality.

And this is why importance is placed on becoming good and loving, and not on academic development. Many saints of the past were said to be uneducated and illiterate. It's worth noting that Jesus didn't bother making any philosophical arguments for the existence of God. He did not appeal to logic or reasoning, because only faith in God leads you to God, and faith comes from your heart, not your rational faculties. This is a point nicely made by the 19th Century Danish philosopher Søren Kierkegaard when he said, "*To have faith is to lose your mind and to win God.*" Similarly, Jesus refers to the importance of the heart, and not the mind, for understanding his message:

> "*This is why I speak to them in parables: Though seeing, they do not see; though hearing, they do not hear or understand. In them is fulfilled the prophecy of Isaiah: 'You will be ever hearing but never understanding; you will be ever seeing but never perceiving. For this people's heart has become calloused; they hardly hear with their ears, and they have closed their eyes. Otherwise they might see with their eyes, hear with their ears, understand with their hearts and turn, and I would heal them'*" (Matt 13:13-15).

It is the heart that understands, not the mind. All beliefs are the result of an internal resonation with the message of that belief, meaning it is your heart that determines what you *can* believe and thus what you *do* believe. And only a certain type of heart can understand Jesus' message.

Hence someone can hear the great spiritual teachings without understanding them, as they may lack the correct psychological disposition to do so. Such an understanding is not based on intelligence. The message has to resonate. And many people dismiss the teachings because they don't resonate with them, but, of course, that doesn't make them untrue. This point is brought out by Buddha in the sixteenth chapter of the Lotus Sutra where he says:

> "*Good men, if there are living beings who come to me, I employ my Buddha eye to observe their faith and to see if*

*their other faculties are keen or dull, and then depending upon how receptive they are to salvation, I appear in different places and preach to them under different names, and describe the length of time during which my teachings will be effective."*[29]

The inability to understand the spiritual teachings is demonstrated by the Pharisees and Sadducees in the narrative of the New Testament. They encountered Jesus' teachings and possibly witnessed his various miracles too, or at least heard testimony of them, but they still denied Jesus as a messiah and rejected his teachings, despite him fulfilling the prophecies of their own scriptures (the Old Testament). This was because they lacked the psychological disposition to appreciate and understand the teachings.

Spiritual philosophy teaches you to be good; goodness being that which leads to salvation. (What it means to be good is explained in my other title *The Moral Law*.) But goodness is a prerequisite for the ability to understand the spiritual teachings—the teachings themselves do not lead to goodness. A fitting example to demonstrate this is Prince Duryodhana in the Mahabharata epic. He was the cousin of the crown prince Yudhisthira, who was considered the epitome of righteousness. Duryodhana, on the other hand, was evil in disposition, and was desperate for personal power and glory. In attempts to assume the position of crown prince for himself, he concocted devious plans to remove Yudhisthira. This eventually resulted in the Kurukshetra war that formed the finale of the epic. Prior to this war, there is an incident where, in dialogue with Krishna, Duryodhana explains that he has heard the spiritual teachings, as he grew up in the same

---

[29] *The Lotus Sutra: Translations from the Asian Classics*, translated by Burton Watson. (New York: Columbia University Press, 1994), 226.

palace as Yudhisthira and thus had the same education as him. But Duryodhana goes on to explain that, even though he knows the difference between good and bad, he cannot help but act in a bad way, as he is compelled to do so by the impulses within him—it is his nature to act in such a way.

So Duryodhana had only a superficial academic understanding of spiritual philosophy and lacked the resonation with the teachings—his behaviour was not reflective of a true understanding. Simply understanding what is right and wrong is not enough. One has to *feel* it too. The mere academic understanding of it is insufficient to actualise the process that it articulates. It is a state of being and belief (faith) rather than a mere intellectual acceptance.

A superficial understanding of spiritual philosophy is not its purpose. Some make it into an academic subject and theorise and philosophise over it, but it then becomes an unproven doctrine like any other and consequently cannot be considered superior to any other theistic or non-theistic doctrine. Because, the superiority of spiritual philosophy lies in its testability, so without testing it, it cannot be proven and therefore cannot be argued for. The purpose of spiritual philosophy is to put the teachings into practice and thereby *know* the reality by experiencing the reality, in the same way that the purpose of a bike is to be ridden. Sure, you can use the bike as a coat-hanger, but that is not its inherent purpose, and the bike is wasted in such use. This idea is depicted by an account given in the Kalama Sutta, a Buddhist text. The people of Kalama were unsure what the true spiritual teachings were, as they had been bombarded by many so-called spiritual teachers who presented conflicting doctrines whilst claiming authority and expertise. When Buddha visited Kalama, he presented his teaching, but the people of Kalama told him they were confused as to which of the many teachings they had heard was the true teaching, to which Buddha gave the following response:

> "*Do not go upon what has been acquired by repeated hearing; nor upon tradition; nor upon rumour; nor upon what is in a scripture; nor upon surmise; nor upon an axiom; nor upon specious reasoning; nor upon a bias toward a notion that has been pondered over; nor upon another's seeming ability; nor upon the consideration, 'The monk is our teacher.' Kalamas, when you yourselves know: 'These things are good; these things are not blameable; these things are praised by the wise; undertaken and observed, these things lead to benefit and happiness,' enter on and abide in them.*"[30]

He further emphasises this point by saying,

> "*My words should be accepted by the wise, not out of regard for me, but after due investigation—just as gold is accepted as true only after heating, cutting and rubbing.*"[31]

(As a side note, one can learn from a textbook the language to describe the taste of ice-cream, but without the experience of eating ice-cream, their description is just hearsay—they do not *know* the taste of ice-cream and are simply parroting information handed down to them by those who do know it through experience. And, of course, it is better to be a person who eats the ice-cream but can't describe it in language than a person who never eats the ice-cream but can describe it in language. The former is

---

30 *Kalama Sutta: The Buddha's Charter of Free Enquiry* (WH 8), translated by Soma Thera. (Kandy: Buddhist Publication Society, 1981).

31 Embar Krishnamacharya, *Tattvasaṅgraha of Śāntarakṣita: With the Commentary of Kamalaśīla. Ed. with an Introduction in Sanskrit.* (Baroda: Central Library, 1926), GOS, Gaekwad's Oriental Series 30–31 v. 3587.

a Truth-seer, the latter a teacher. The teacher becomes a religious missionary who spends his whole time describing how the finger points out the moon without ever looking at the moon himself. This is an idea nicely brought out by George Bernard Shaw, the Irish playwright [born in 1856], when he said, *"Those that can, do; those that can't, teach."* Note, saints [sages, *yogis*, *rishis*, etc.] are not considered teachers but guides, as spiritual philosophy emphasises experience, not academia, and the spiritual teachings are aimed at making you a Truth-seer, not a teacher.)

But it's not only about being good. It's also about timing and spiritual competency. I first heard a talk on spiritual philosophy when I was about fifteen years old. After the talk, I could not recall one thing that had been said; I had not understood anything. Not only was this due to a lack of resonation, but I had not concentrated during the talk either. My mind had wandered off and could not focus on the message. It's not that the message was overly complex or beyond my intellectual capacity, but rather the psychological disposition to hear and understand this message (i.e. spiritual competency) was absent, and hence there was no (conscious or subconscious) interest in picking up the message.

You may be reading this now and rejecting it. If so, that is because it does not resonate with you—it doesn't *feel* right. But this is the case with anyone who rejects any ideology. The process by which one "chooses" the ideologies he subscribes to is based on internal resonation (whether they *feel* right to him).

But can one adopt faith in a proposition without truly resonating with it? This question refers to Pascal's Wager, an argument made by the 17th Century French philosopher and mathematician Blaise Pascal, which, put simply, claims that it is more rational to accept the existence of God than reject it, as one stands to lose more by rejecting it should it be true than by accepting it should it be false.

In formulating this argument, Pascal provides the anecdote of a young man who claims that he simply cannot believe, as he does not resonate with the message. Pascal argues that the young man should adopt the belief regardless, as he benefits from doing so. But this is a poor argument, because belief is based on resonation. If you do not have the resonation, then you cannot *truly* believe; you are just fooling yourself and engaging in self-deception.

And the process of salvation is a mental one, meaning it requires a certain psychological disposition and state of mind. (Salvation is a state of existence and not a temporal place that can be visited by adopting certain traits and behaviours.) Thus acquisition of faith is *not* an intellectual determination but a state of being that transpires once spiritual competency dawns. And this dawns when certain spiritual criteria have been met. It is a science, a process of cause and effect. And the starting point is to be good. So Pascal was wrong to advocate adoption of a fake belief.

In fact, "fake belief" is an oxymoron. It is not mentally possible, as you can only believe in that which you intuit (feel) is true. The ideologies you subscribe to have to line up with your internal psychological disposition. That is to say, there has to be a resonation with the ideology—you can't convince yourself to believe something that doesn't feel right.

Thus faith is something that is intrinsic to one's nature. Faith cannot be taught or induced in a person through reasoning, just as a passive nature cannot be induced in a lion, as the lion's nature is to be aggressive. So spiritual teachers (or guides), unlike religious missionaries, do not waste time trying to convert non-believers into believers, but only instruct spiritual aspirants on the path and lay out the teachings for those who are drawn to them and ready for them. This is analogous to how advanced mathematics is taught to those who have an interest in and competency for it, and not given to or forced upon five-year old children who are incapable of comprehending it. Hence spiritual philosophy is considered esoteric knowledge—only some can understand it. But it is applicable to everyone, like the way in which everyone is governed by the laws of physics even though only some can understand or appreciate them.

This same principle also applies to lower knowledge of the external world. Ability and competency in acquiring this "knowledge" varies, with some people demonstrating a higher capacity for certain disciplines, such as science, language, art, or music, than others. Some do not have the ability to appreciate fine art, and some do not have the ability to appreciate advanced mathematical theorems. So each person has an intrinsic ability and competency to understand certain matters but not others, and this intrinsic ability enables them to execute the specific role assigned to them by the cosmic creator (more on this shortly).

## Why Some Believe and Others Don't

The proverb, "you can lead a horse to water, but you can't make it drink" is applicable to belief. You can lead a person to an idea, but you can't make them believe in it. This is especially relevant to the question of God. Belief in God cannot be an intellectual determination, because you cannot reason your way to the belief in it. The Katha Upanishad affirms this by saying: *"[God] is smaller than the smallest yet larger than the largest"* (Katha Upanishad 1:2:20).

This statement is a logical paradox and demonstrates that reason does *not* reflect reality. It also shows that God is not subject to logic and thus cannot be known through logic; God defies and transcends logic, and all laws of logic are negated by God. Swami Yogeshwarananda says that this verse is used to stun you into mental silence, and thereby indirectly reveal the way to God.

This is because all intellection uses reason and logic, but reason and logic cannot make sense of this verse—it cannot be conceptualised. So when you hear this verse, reason and logic, which are mental activities, stop, and you are dumbstruck or shocked into a state of mental silence.

All philosophical arguments for the existence of God (such as ontological, contingency, cosmological, and teleological arguments) are redundant because God is not a philosophy but a state of existence. Spiritual philosophy ignores such arguments, as the spiritual teachings only show you the *way* to God, and do not offer philosophical/logical proof of God (because you can't prove the unprovable). This is also why Krishna nor Buddha nor Jesus bothered with such arguments.

So the question "Is it rational to believe in God?" is an oxymoron, because belief in God is based on faith and not reason (a philosophical view known as fideism). Theistic philosophers desperately attempt to provide rational arguments for the existence of and belief in God, as seemingly they do not want to be considered "irrational", but there is an intrinsic futility in their endeavour. As soon as you try to reason your way to God, you turn God into a philosophy, and reason becomes your God—you demonstrate faith in reason and not God. And note, when specifically asked, Jesus said that the greatest commandment is: *"Love the Lord your God with all your heart and with all your soul and with all your mind"* (Matt 22:37). He emphasised a mental state rather than an intellectual pursuit. Thus it is love, not reason, that takes you to salvation. And love is not a product of reason; nobody reasons their way to being in love.

But even more generally, philosophical arguments are redundant, because, as mentioned earlier, they are all founded on an unprovable axiom (faith). And it's apparent that logic and reason do not, on their own, lead to the ideologies that one subscribes to.

If they do, that's only because the person *values* logic and reason, and has a personal faith in it. *Why* they have this faith or *where* this faith comes from are interesting questions, but seemingly the same processes that lead to religious faith can be used to explain faith in reason and science, such as indoctrination, socio-cultural conditioning, conformity, desire to be on the side of "the intelligent", and so on. Perhaps even they idolise certain logical empiricists and want to follow in their footsteps. (The New Atheist movement is a religion like any other, with its priests being the logical empiricists who make unprovable metaphysical claims about the nature of reality.)

So people aren't swayed by logical arguments; they are led by their faith. Therefore, it's futile to try to convince someone to adopt an ideology by using a logical argument. Here are some examples to demonstrate this point...

Peter Singer, a contemporary Australian philosopher, created the Drowning Child thought experiment: if a person has a moral obligation to rescue a drowning child when there is no significant risk or cost to themselves to do so, then they should have a moral obligation to save a starving child on the other side of the world by donating money to the necessary charity. The only major difference between the two scenarios, he argues, is one of distance, which seems inadequate to justify a difference in moral obligation. However, we know from sociological studies that most people aren't swayed to donate to charities based on such philosophical arguments, but instead are swayed by an experience that triggers a powerful emotional response in them. This is why charities do not lay out philosophical arguments in their advertisements but use graphic imagery of malnourished children in apparent suffering; the charities know that this is a much more effective way of getting people to donate money.

Similarly, veganism is an ideology and way of life that is growing in the Western world. Many philosophically minded vegans present logical arguments to promote veganism. For instance, they argue that it is irrational to deem it immoral to kill and eat a human *if* you do not deem it immoral to kill and eat an animal. Such arguments are designed to reveal a philosophical inconsistency in your reasoning, but they do not seem to convince people to adopt veganism. And understandably so. Why should it matter to someone that they hold philosophically inconsistent views? This would only matter if they valued reason. But perhaps they don't. And clearly, people *can* hold inconsistent views—it is not an impossibility. This is because views (or propositions) can be based not just on reason but also on attitudes, feelings, and intuitions, and there are no laws of consistency when it comes to these. For instance, a person's reason may conclude that it is wrong to be deceitful, but their intuition may conclude otherwise, thus enabling them to tell a lie. Simply understanding the inconsistency is insufficient to modify one's behaviour. Consequently, regarding veganism, people are generally convinced much more by graphic imagery of animals being mistreated and slaughtered, as such information triggers powerful emotional responses that can motivate change in behaviour.

And lastly, Alan Kurdi was a three-year-old boy who drowned in the sea in 2015 whilst he and his family were escaping the Syrian war to seek refuge in a foreign land. His body was found lying face-down on a Turkish beach, and a photograph of this emerged and became front page news. The picture had a huge impact on people, and somewhat led to a change in general opinion about the refugee crisis from Syria. This is the power that such an image has. Rationally, people should be swayed more by an article detailing the deaths of thousands of people in the war than the image of one dead boy, but the image was able to provoke a response that such articles could not. And this is because images, unlike articles, resonate with people, and they can personally relate to them. Perhaps they see their own child in that situation, which triggers a deep emotional response.

These examples suggest that most people are swayed by personal stories that strike a chord and not by meaningless philosophical argumentation. And this may be the means by which all ideologies are formed.

Hence people are more likely to be converted to theism through testimonies and heart-touching stories from converts, who describe theism changing their lives for the better and bringing meaning and purpose to them, than by some fancy philosophical argument for the existence of God, such as an ontological argument. Such philosophical arguments are impotent, invisible weapons that academics use to fight each other—the arguments don't actually do any damage.

It would be surprising to find someone who'd converted to a particular religion, political ideology, or veganism based on argumentation. Though, it can *appear* this way, as people may claim (ignorantly) that they were convinced by such argumentation.

As mentioned earlier, there are various factors that determine whether one is drawn to an ideology or not, but argumentation on its own cannot be one of them. Because, if two conceivable propositions are being considered, then argumentation alone is insufficient to lead to adopting one over the other; there must be underlying psychological factors that determine why someone is drawn to one side over the other. So there is an intrinsic futility to debates, because the psychological disposition to support one side or the other is already present, meaning no one is convinced by the arguments per se; they just use the arguments to justify their preconceived position. That is, a person does not form a belief on the back of an argument but rather adopts the argument that supports their underlying belief. (Of course, the position/belief may be subconscious and not openly acknowledged by the person prior to hearing the argument, so the *false* notion that "the argument caused my belief" may arise.)

Hence general philosophy is a futile subject; it is meaningless academia that offers no practical utility. Spiritual philosophy is equally meaningless as an academic subject, but it does offer practical utility in that it provides a process that can be actualised and realised: While the ultimate conclusion of general philosophy is "I know nothing and I cannot know anything", the ultimate conclusion of spiritual philosophy is "I know nothing but I *can* know everything".

And as spiritual philosophy teaches you to drop all your ideologies and to not seek an identity, it leads you to a non-partisan state with impartiality and indifference. And relevantly, Buddha teaches indifference as one of the four key virtues (*Brahmaviharas*) for enlightenment.

When you drop all ideologies, you have no enemies. Because, when you adopt an ideology, you automatically oppose those who reject it. But the saint is a friend to everyone, as he does not oppose any ideas; he understands the futility of all of them and thus treats them all equally.

And saints and spiritual aspirants work alone. They do not belong to a group or institution, because they do not subscribe to any ideology or doctrine, and thereby have nothing in common with anyone. This was the founding principle underlying the ancient monastic tradition of India, which resulted in monasteries and hermitages (known as ashrams) facilitating independent living with an individually tailored spiritual pursuit.

Hindu philosophy states that the subconscious of the mind is constituted of numerous impressions (known in Sanskrit as *vasanas* and *samskaras*). These impressions include one's likes and dislikes (*ragas* and *dweshas*), their attachments (*moha*), their desires (*kama*), and their emotional tendencies. And these determine the ideologies that a person subscribes to.

A person may have a subconscious attraction to a speaker, which draws them into the speaker's ideology (as the two go together); so the attraction, not the content of the ideology, is doing the work. Or perhaps the person is drawn to the group of that ideology. This does appear to play a role and is suggested by the observation that members of a specific ideology tend to have similar traits and share unrelated ideologies. For instance, politically and economically left-leaning people disproportionately favour ideologies like climate change, veganism, abortion, and secularism, even though these are typically unrelated. Also, younger adults tend to lean towards left-wing politics and socialist values, even though there is no obvious connection between youth and such a leaning. However, once this becomes the position of the young, future young people will be drawn to it, as they associate with being young and consequently adopt the typical values connected to youth. (Of course, not all, and some become non-conformists, but as mentioned earlier, most people have an urge to fit in and be part of the majority or at least conform with their group.) In this manner, the ideology becomes a self-perpetuating identity of that group and thus becomes difficult to dislodge.

Of course, this is a gross generalisation, and some people will have a unique composition of views and cannot be categorised easily. But it seems the majority of people who identify with a group demonstrate loyalty to and conformity with the group. This results in an automatic adoption of all the core values, behaviours, and ideologies of that group (herd mentality). For example, certain professions are favoured by some ethnic groups in a society but not others. Also, attire is linked to ideology whereby people subscribing to a particular ideology tend to dress in a similar manner, even though there is no obligation to do so. This is seen in various religious, cultural, and socio-political groups, which allows for the correct identification of the group's ideology based on attire alone.[32] This is a peculiar phenomenon considering that, typically, there is no logical association between the ideology and the attire (or other traits). A good example of this is body art. Tattoos and body piercings are significantly more common in certain activist groups than the general population, despite there being no obvious connection between these lifestyle choices and the ideology of that group. Basically, people tend to connect and associate with a group and *then* formulate their core values, behaviours, and ideologies. This human tendency to categorise oneself appears to be driven by a desire to belong to and be part of something.

So one develops an identity and then adopts the values and ideologies of that identity. And evidently, most people stick with the identity that they are born with and conditioned into, whether it be religious or political. This suggests that it is one's nature that draws them to a specific ideology, not argumentation. The way this is achieved is by the underlying nature creating *desires*, and these (for whatever reason) pushing a person into a specific ideology.

Bear in mind, we are talking about strong ideologies and beliefs here, not mere acceptances. Of course, one can subscribe to certain historical explanations, logical proofs, or scientific claims based on reasoning, but these are not necessarily irreversibly held with strong conviction. Beliefs, on the other hand, typically *are*, and they become part of one's identity.

---

[32] Perhaps this is why Adam and Eve were naked in the Garden of Eden—to represent a pure and unconditioned state. And saints, unlike priests and religious missionaries, do not have specific attire or a uniform; they dress in a variety of ways, with some even choosing to go naked (although note, nakedness does not necessarily imply sainthood, as people adopt nakedness for a multitude of reasons).

Even though the cause-effect relationship between two ideologies can be contested (for example, "socialism leads to acceptance of climate change" versus "acceptance of climate change leads to socialism"), there *is* a relationship (or at least a correlation). And it seems reasonable to presume that one ideology has led to the other, suggesting ideologies come from other ideologies rather than argumentation...

This proposal can be represented by an analogy used by Descartes in formulating the *Cogito*. Descartes presented the example of a basket of apples in which some of the apples are rotten. As rot spreads, the only way to be sure that any apple isn't rotten is to empty the basket and inspect each apple individually. Essentially, he was claiming that all ideologies must be stripped from one's psyche and individually re-examined to ensure they have not been erected on the back of underlying (and prior) rotten ideologies. (The analogy of rot spreading is a fitting way of thinking about how beliefs accumulate within a person's psyche. Of course, herd mentality is an alternative explanation, but an underlying axiom, which spreads like rot and forms the basis of all one's ideologies, appears to contribute. But remember, no axiom, apart from the *Cogito*, can be justified.)

As said, you and your mind are a bundle of impressions (*vasanas* and *samskaras*), and these impressions determine your beliefs, values, desires, and likes and dislikes. But where do these impressions come from? They come from your experiences (and subsequent mental conditioning). And this process is predictable and inevitable because it is based on cause-and-effect. Everything you know (or think you know) is based on information that has been presented to you via your experiences. So you cannot help but be who you are, as you are the inevitable consequence of your experiences—experiences that you do not control. You are the result of certain spiritual laws that operate in the universe. This idea is known as spiritual determinism...

Spiritual determinism (or psychological determinism) is the view that all character traits and operations of the mind (plus beliefs, feelings, emotions, desires, and actions) are the inevitable result of the mind's experiences and conditioning, and *not* biological factors or genetic predisposition. This is also known as *karma*. As one's experiences are outside of their control, they have no choice (or free-will) over what they think, feel, and do. For example, a violent nature is the result of previous traumatic experiences. In Buddhist philosophy, the laws of *karma* exist and operate independent of God. Whereas, in Hindu philosophy, spiritual determinism is part of "theological determinism" whereby a cosmic super-intelligence and creator, known as *Ishvara*, orchestrates the whole operation of *karma*.

So theological determinism is the view that everything is pre-determined by the will of God—there is no individual free-will. This is the position of spiritual philosophy, which likens creation to a pre-scripted Divine play in which all beings perform a role assigned to them. The spiritual error (fall) occurs when a person develops a (false) sense of ego and erroneously believes that they are the cause of their actions and have agency over them. Theological determinism is also adopted by some religious sects like Calvinism (a major branch of Protestant Christianity).

In this sense, everything you are, everything you do, and everything you think you know, are all because the cosmic super-intelligence has ordained it so and conditioned you accordingly. He wants it that way. This is not dissimilar to Descartes' Evil Demon who presents you with an illusion that conditions all your thoughts and beliefs: If the Evil Demon wants you, for instance, to believe in God, he will give you the necessary experiences in order to do so; if he doesn't want you to believe in God, he will give you the necessary experiences (or lack thereof) to disbelieve.

## *The Case for the Non-natural*

Is there evidence for non-natural phenomena to support the existence of God and undermine the doctrine of materialism? Well, it depends on what is meant by "evidence". Many non-naturalists provide observations and data suggestive of reincarnation, out-of-body experiences, extra-sensory perception, ghosts, or miracles, but whether you choose to accept these as evidence depends on your psychological disposition and bias.

Clearly, the current academic and scientific institutions reject such phenomena. And seemingly, this is because they threaten the foundation on which these institutions are built, namely materialism. That is to say, information that threatens the foundation of an institution is disregarded or conveniently ignored by that institution. No surprise there. It's a similar thing to an institutional religion rejecting any ideas that threaten its own dogmas: (a practice adopted by the Catholic Church through the Inquisition in medieval times).

The rejection can be intentional or subconscious... Fraud, hoaxes, and suppression of evidence are done with an agenda, but sometimes evidence is unintentionally rejected and explained away using some form of mental justification (a process called denial). Both processes may contribute to societal scepticism about supernatural phenomena.

The current principle governing scientific investigation is methodological naturalism, which is based in materialism. This is now also invoked for historical investigation, seemingly due to the power and influence that science has recently acquired. And, of course, this has practical utility. For instance, when investigating a crime scene, methodological naturalism is invoked, as we expect a naturalistic cause for such an event. This is because we use a principle of induction here—we recognise that such events typically have naturalistic explanations. However, we *cannot* assume naturalistic causation for fundamental existential issues, such as the origin of consciousness, the origin of the cosmos, and the origin of species, because these are one-off events that have never been observed and thus cannot be compared to other phenomena we know of. So a principle of induction cannot be invoked to explain these events, and consequently non-material causation cannot be considered inferior to material causation for explaining them.

But even in considering recent historical events, for which we *can* use a principle of induction, methodological naturalism is only a tool that offers practical utility. It does not offer certainty. Hence you can never exclude non-material explanations for any phenomena. Nonetheless, we typically use a "burden of proof" threshold for accepting material explanations, and this seems reasonable.

But as Hume pointed out with the problem of induction, just because things behave in a certain way now does not mean they will behave in this way in the future. And similarly, we can apply this principle retrospectively: just because things behave in a certain way now does not mean they have always behaved in this way; perhaps we can call this the problem of reverse induction.

So the claim "miracles do not happen now and therefore miracles have never happened in the past" is an unreasonable deduction—there is no logical inference to get from the premise to the conclusion. Science cannot make this claim either (because it is untestable). A probability argument could be invoked here to argue "miracles do not happen now and therefore they *probably* haven't happened in the past". But this is tricky territory because the claim "miracles do not happen now" is not provable (as you cannot prove a negative), and so what this claim really implies is "I don't believe in miracles" or "I have never personally experienced a miracle". But remember, your personal experiences, and what you personally believe, are not a reflection of reality. The point being: do not make metaphysical claims about the nature and operations of the universe based on your personal experiences. Just because you have not personally experienced a miracle, and just because the people in whom you put your faith preach that miracles do not happen, does not mean miracles do not happen or have never happened.

You should be open-minded to any explanation. Of course, naturalistic explanations will oftentimes suffice, but there are cases where the possibility of miracles should be entertained. For instance, there are numerous cases in the literature of spontaneous healings wherein people with terminal and incurable diseases are mysteriously cured—neither doctors nor science can give a medical explanation for these cases. So in such cases, it is wise to remain open-minded and agnostic on whether the remission of the disease was a miracle or not.

Similarly, if you witness a strange phenomenon, like a man walking on water or healing someone or materialising a solid object through mentation, then you should remain open-minded here and not shut the door on the possibility of supernatural causation. In the Eastern traditions, such phenomena are recognised as possible, and the abilities to perform such acts are known as *siddhis*. Due to the current paradigm of materialism in the West, such phenomena are typically rejected by the masses. (The 2009 "What do Philosophers Believe" survey by Chalmers and Bourget, which assessed philosophers' views, found that a minority subscribed to non-naturalism [25.9%] and almost half subscribed to naturalism [49.8%]. [24.3% selected the "other" option]. Also, the survey found physicalism [56.3%] was more than twice as popular as non-physicalism [27.1%].[33] The updated 2020 survey revealed a modest narrowing of the gap [naturalism at 49.4% and non-naturalism at 30.3%; physicalism at 51.6% and non-physicalism at 31.9%], perhaps indicating the early stages of a paradigm shift.[34]) Of course, a naturalistic explanation can be offered for the observation of a man walking on water (perhaps just beneath the surface is a glass plank on which he is balancing), but the idea is to remain open to the *possibility* of there being a non-natural cause. As soon as you negate this possibility, you limit yourself and subscribe to an ideology, namely materialism.

A materialist can, and typically does, offer a material explanation for any unusual phenomenon. And, as a last resort, he can always suggest that the experiencer of the phenomenon (even if it is himself) is hallucinating: this can never be disproved (and therefore a miracle, like anything else, can never be proven). Though, such a claim would only highlight his prejudice and close-mindedness (the opposite of what a scientist is supposed to possess).

And this is the problem with "evidence". The same data and observations are interpreted in one way by one group, and another way by another group, with both groups basing their interpretations on preconceived ideas. For example, if you are a materialist, you will always offer naturalistic explanations for phenomena. Whereas, if you are a non-materialist, you might offer non-naturalistic explanations.

---

33 David Bourget and David Chalmers, "What do Philosophers Believe?" *Philosophical Studies: An International Journal for Philosophy in the Analytic Tradition.* Vol. 170, No. 3 (September 2014): 465–500.

34 David Bourget and David Chalmers, "Philosophers on Philosophy: The 2020 PhilPapers Survey," *Philosophers' Imprint.* Vol. 23, Issue 1, No. 11 (2023). doi: https://doi.org/10.3998/phimp.2109

Many people say that there is no solid evidence for miracles, because if there was, the scientific institution and media would provide it. However, it is not inconceivable that data and observations suggestive of the non-natural are deliberately suppressed and hidden from you. This might sound conspiratorial, but this is seemingly the way the world operates. Even parents conceal certain information from their children, as they want to condition them in a specific way. So it's not a stretch to imagine that the controlling authorities (or the state) do this with their subjects.

Societies typically run on propaganda and control the beliefs of their people by providing specific information. It is no surprise that people in communist regimes tend to support communism, and people in capitalist societies tend to support capitalism. People from both sides shout from the rooftops that *their* ideology is superior, not realising that they are simply a conditioned product of propaganda—had they been born on the other side, they would be championing that other side's view. Obviously, this is seen in religion too, where the majority of religious people simply adopt the religion they are born into and then champion it. But this is also the case with materialism and atheism (positive atheism), which can be seen as religions (as they make unprovable metaphysical claims), and these are now the doctrines of the West, promoted by secular, scientific regimes. Many proponents of these ideologies shout from the rooftops that their position is superior to the alternative, without realising that their position is merely the inevitable product of their society's propaganda.

Up until a few centuries ago, propaganda was used to develop support for the Church, which had power and control over what people believed. Today, the Church has been replaced by the scientific institution and secular government, at least in the Western world, whereby an ideology of materialism is promoted. The propaganda we see today is used to support this ideology.

While religious indoctrination is typically supported by the historical method and historical evidence (like relics, archaeology, narrative, and testimony), materialistic indoctrination is typically supported by the scientific method and scientific evidence. Indeed, a few centuries ago in Western Europe, Christian doctrine was promoted as fact, using historical evidence to support it, and consequently the masses lapped it up. Today, however, in the West, the doctrine of materialism is promoted as fact, using scientific evidence to support it, and consequently it's lapped up by the masses (or at least by most who aren't exposed to other views). So there is no significant difference here. Both groups have fallen victim to indoctrination—they simply accept what they are told. (Note, neither the historical method nor the scientific method can be deemed superior as a source of knowledge.)

So people may have freed themselves from the cage of religion, but they have stumbled into the cage of materialism. And this is because of the human tendency to want some ideology to latch on to—people feel more comfortable being trapped in an ideological cage (being doctrinally institutionalised) than being free of all ideologies.

But belief in non-naturalism or miracles can result in problems too. People can be enticed by such, and this can lead them astray. The spiritual path does not advocate the acquisition of *siddhis*, as these distract from the true purpose of the spiritual path, which is experience of the reality (salvation). This truth is demonstrated in Chapter 4 of the Gospel of Matthew (verses 1-9) where the Devil tempts Jesus with offerings of glory but Jesus rejects them. (Note, saints and messiahs are said to possess the power to perform miracles; however, they use this only for a higher purpose as ordained by the cosmic will, and do not use it to fulfil personal desires, such as acquiring personal wealth and glory, which is what the Devil offered Jesus.)

Black magic and tantric practices, which are mentioned in the Vedas, are only desired by unspiritual characters.[35] They should be discouraged and not promoted in a society (but this doesn't give cause to actively disbelieve in them).

In this sense, the belief in miracles may not be beneficial to a society, as it is not necessary for spiritual growth and conversely can impede it. So the cosmic super-intelligence, who controls what you (and society in general) believe, may see fit to hide such information from you. (Remember, it is the cosmic super-intelligence who is the ultimate authority and cause of all your beliefs; propaganda from the state is just the seeming means He uses to achieve this.)

## The Message of Spiritual Philosophy

Spiritual philosophy describes two phenomena: the reality and the unreality. The reality is God, and the unreality is you and the universe. This forms the Eastern basis of dualism. But truly speaking, the unreality does not exist; it is an illusion of sorts. Thus only the reality *is*. This is the Eastern notion of non-dualism, which is also known as *advaita*.

To describe the relationship between the reality and the unreality, the Upanishads give a fitting analogy of a rope on the ground in twilight being mistaken for a snake...

Only the rope exists, and the snake does not have a real existence. Though, the snake is a phenomenon that is perceived by

---

35 The Vedas are a body of religious texts associated with Hinduism. They talk of practices that are unspiritual in nature and opposed to the doctrine of salvation. Thus a distinction should be made between the Upanishads, which are a scripture, and the Vedas. Be aware that the Upanishads have been arbitrarily incorporated into the Vedas and considered "part" of the Vedas in an attempt to offer the Vedas credibility. The two should not be conflated, as they have different origins and purposes, and they focus on and speak of different things.

you—it is a misperception. So there is a duality of sorts—the rope *and* the snake. Now, the snake's existence is completely dependent on the rope: it emerges from the rope and the rope is its basis and substratum. But the rope is not dependent on the snake in any way, and once the rope has been discerned, the snake disappears forever and only the rope remains. This is non-duality. It is not that the rope comes into existence: the rope always existed—it was just hidden by the snake. This idea is also brought out in what Swami Yogeshwarananda says is the most philosophical verse in the Bhagavad Gita: *"The unreal has no existence, the real never ceases to exist; the truth about both has been seen by the knowers of the Truth"* (Bhagavad Gita 2:16).[36]

The relationship between the reality and the unreality refers to the mystery of creation. The Upanishads present various models of creation. One model claims that the physical universe is created first and then individual minds (souls) are created in separate acts. This model accommodates the Genesis account of creation from the Bible and gives rise to Western-philosophy dualism (explained in a moment). A second model claims that minds are created first and from the expansion of these, the universe arises—the universe is the result of mental processes. This model leads to a metaphysical worldview known as idealism (explained in a moment). A third model proposes that you (your mind) and the universe emerge simultaneously (and together) in a mysterious process where you both depend on each other to exist, like how in a dream, the dreamer and the dream world emerge together and enable each other to exist. This model, like the first, gives rise to Western-philosophy dualism. (The dream analogy can be used for dualism as well as idealism.) And a fourth model espouses

---

36 Translation by Swami Yogeshwarananda.

non-creationism, which is the idea that creation is a myth and that both you and the universe are inexplicable phenomena that do not really exist.

Interestingly, spiritual philosophy does not commit to one specific metaphysical model, as it does not want you to subscribe to a specific ideology, and wants you to remain open-minded. These models are only presented as a means to pointing out the reality, like a finger pointing out the moon. This is so because the reality can only be known through non-perceptual, non-mental experience. It cannot be explained to you in words or shown to you. So these models only have a practical utility. They lead you to experience the reality; they in themselves cannot reveal the reality.

Also, as Swami Yogeshwarananda says, none of these models are true, because they are constructs of the human mind and thus are part of the unreality. There is no true cause of an unreality: the snake is not a truly real phenomenon and thus cannot have a truly real cause. So the creation models are only human constructions devised to lead you *out* of the unreality and *in* to the reality.

And the relationship between the reality and the unreality is peculiar and cannot be explained, perceived, or conceptualised. But it can be known through non-perceptual, non-mental experience. Hence the models are only used to explain that there *is* a peculiar relationship and thereby offer a way of *thinking about* the relationship for the purpose of distinguishing the reality from the unreality. Until you are told by someone that it is not a snake but a rope, you will keep your distance and remain in fear. But once instructed and encouraged to take a closer look, you can realise it is a rope and not a snake. Similarly, the scriptures and spiritual teachers (or guides) come and tell you that what you are perceiving in your current state is the unreality, so take a closer look and experience the reality instead.

Of course, you can hypothesise and argue over why and how the snake has emerged and its relationship to the rope, though there is an obvious futility to this: To argue over whether the mistake arises due to dim light, the formation of the rope, faulty vision of the perceiver, or the perceiver's underlying fear of snakes, is a waste of time.

General philosophy fumbles around trying to work out the cause and the nature of the snake, whereas spiritual philosophy ignores this and says, go closer and have a look at the snake and thereby experience the rope instead; once you do this, all questions about the snake are answered. This is also why Buddha taught that, if you get shot with a poisoned arrow, then you should not worry about the origins of the arrow, the type of bow used, or the character of the shooter; instead, you should just focus on removing the arrow.[37] I.e. don't concern yourself with the *cause* of the problem, but concern yourself with the *solution* to the problem.

Remember, spiritual philosophy provides the process by which complete knowledge of everything can be acquired. This includes knowledge of yourself and the nature of reality. And this is achieved by looking inwards, because the secret of reality lies *within* you: Jesus said, *"the Kingdom of Heaven is within you"* (Luke 17:21 [KJV]).[38] The spiritual enquiry starts with Descartes' *Cogito* but then goes inwards to address the fundamental nature of your soul, not outwards to address the objects or operations of the external world. And it is this internal enquiry that leads to the experience, and consequently knowledge, of the reality.

---

[37] Buddha gives this teaching in a parable which is found in the Culamalukya Sutta (MN 63).

[38] Cf. the Ancient Greek aphorism "know thyself". This is the first of many maxims encountered in the Temple of Apollo at Delphi, as it was the first of the three main maxims inscribed above the entrance.

While the relationship between the reality and the unreality refers to the mystery of creation, the relationship between you and the universe refers to the fundamental nature of the mind. In Western philosophy, there are typically three dominant and competing models for explaining this relationship: dualism, idealism, and physicalism.

Physicalism, like materialism, is a metaphysical philosophy that asserts that everything is physical and can be reduced to physical matter and physical (or naturalistic) processes, meaning mind emerges from the body and is dependent on the body. Idealism is a range of diverse metaphysical views that (mostly) assert that everything is mental, meaning mind is the primary and fundamental substance in existence, and the physical universe (including physical bodies) emerges from mind and is dependent on mind—the external physical world is mentally constituted and cannot exist without mind. Solipsism-idealism claims that the world is a creation of *your* mind, analogous to how your mind creates a dream world when you go to sleep and start dreaming—it's all a product of your mind and there is no independent existence of that dream world. Both idealism and physicalism are categorised under monism, also termed "non-dualism" in Western philosophy (different from the Eastern concept of non-dualism), as they claim that there is only one fundamental and primary substance, not two: either mind (idealism) or matter (physicalism).[39]

---

[39] There is a philosophical view known as neutral monism that claims the fundamental essence of reality is neither mental nor physical but a third "neutral" substance. This "third" substance must have creative power and be the cause of the other two, and therefore must be the fundamental reality (God). So this view makes no practical difference to spiritual philosophy. Indeed, in Hindu philosophy, *Brahman* is considered an inconceivable and indescribable transcendental (third) substance, separate from both mind and matter but from which both mind and matter emerge. But because mind and matter are considered an illusion of creation, there are, in reality, not three substances but only one (*Brahman*). We could refer to this as non-triality!

Dualism, on the other hand, claims that there are two primary phenomena: mind and matter—you and the universe, the perceiver and the perceived. So the mind and the body are distinct entities that exist separately and have different points of origin (i.e. the mind does not originate from the physical body). They are not dependent on one another, yet they interact with each other and influence each other (a process known as interactionism in Western philosophy). Dualism typically incorporates the idea of a soul, where the soul can be equated to the mind that exists inside the body but is not caused by the body. This has been described as the "ghost in the machine", where the mind is the ghost and the body is the machine. And this relationship can be analogised to that between a driver and his vehicle...

The physical body is controlled and operated by the mind, like how the vehicle is controlled and operated by the driver—without the driver, the vehicle does not function. And while the vehicle can influence the driver's state (e.g. the comfort of the seats, the fumes from the engine, and the speed at which the vehicle moves can all influence how the driver *feels*), the driver's *existence* is not causally dependent on the vehicle nor emerges from it.

Spiritual philosophy is based on the principle that you are the soul and not the body. The body is just a temporary house that you (or your soul) reside in. And the starting premise of spiritual philosophy is that souls (and mental stuff) are not reducible to physical matter or naturalistic processes. Thus spiritual philosophy negates physicalism (and materialism). But interestingly, spiritual philosophy does not commit to either dualism or idealism, and presents both as viable explanations for the relationship between mind and matter.

This waking state is claimed by spiritual philosophy to be a type of unreality created by your mind. And, similar to a dream, you can wake up from this waking unreality and realise its unreal nature. The waking-up process is what is referred to in religious language as *nirvana*, enlightenment, salvation, liberation, *moksha*, God-experience, and Self-realisation.

Spiritual philosophy asserts that you and the world are part of a myth precipitated by ignorance, an ignorance that gives rise to the misconception that your human existence and the external world form part of the reality. In order to keep the myth going, the truth of reality has to be hidden. (This is a rebuttal to the "Divine Hiddenness Argument" from Western theology/philosophy.)[40] Thus, like Descartes' Evil Demon, a cosmic creator can precipitate false beliefs within you in order to keep you in ignorance and thereby keep the deception going. You might consider this cruel, but it is simply part of the game of creation. Without such measures, creation could not transpire and continue.

Think of a drama... It only occurs because a playwright has written false roles for the actors to assume. The drama relies on the actors playing a false reality; if they do not assume the role of their character, then the drama cannot unfold. The only difference in the analogy is that the actors realise that they are just playing a role assigned to them, whereas you actually think that you are a human with an individual existence. Spiritual philosophy teaches you this error and thereby enables you to detach yourself from the false human individuality that you have assumed. But obviously, if everyone were to do this, there would be problems, so the message is only given to some (or rather, the message is only *heard* by some).

---

40 The Divine Hiddenness Argument essentially claims that, if God exists, then He would make His existence obvious to everyone, but seeing as He does not make His existence obvious to everyone, He does not exist. The argument is used in support of atheism.

So the supreme cosmic intelligence (God) keeps you in darkness for His own purpose—for creation to continue. And that is why intuition does not reflect reality. It only reflects what the Divine playwright *wants* you to believe (in order to carry out the role He has assigned to you). Such an idea is demonstrated by an incident in the Mahabharata episode between Krishna and Sahadeva, the youngest of the five Pandava brothers...

Krishna plays the role of mediator between the two rival camps of the Bharat dynasty, who are contemplating war as a resolution to their conflict. Krishna asks the Pandava brothers, one by one, what their decision on a potential war is. First, Yudhisthira, known for his virtue and integrity, said that he wanted to avoid war and wanted a non-violent solution. The next three brothers said that they wanted to wage war on the rival camp. But when Sahadeva, who was known for his wisdom, was asked, he replied, "*You* are the problem, Krishna, and thus the solution is to tie you up".

Sahadeva wasn't being hostile but was revealing a great spiritual truth by making the metaphysical claim that God the creator is the cause of all events in the universe, in the same way that Shakespeare is the cause of all events that unfold in his plays. Krishna, knowing everything (including what Sahadeva's response would be) asked the question so that this profound answer could be given and subsequently encountered by you here (or in any other place that you may have come across it).

*That knowledge which purifies the mind and heart alone is true knowledge, all else is only a negation of knowledge.*

- Sri Ramakrishna

# INDEX

*advaita*, 81–83
agnostic theism, 48
agnosticism, 46
aliens, belief in, 36
apophenia, 40
Asch Conformity Experiments, 28–29
Asch, Solomon, 29
atheism
   negative atheism. *See* agnosticism
   positive atheism, 46, 48, 79
axiom, 11

bandwagon effect, 27
begging the question, 14

Bhagavad Gita
   ch.2, v.16, 82
   ch.3, v.38, 54
biodiversity, causes of, 32
black swan fallacy, 22, 47
body art, 72
Bourget, David, 77–78
*Brahman*, 18, 85
*Brahmaviharas*, 70
brain in a vat, 21
Brown Simpson, Nicole, 38
Buddha, 59, 61, 66, 70, 84
burden of proof, 48, 76

Calvinism, 74
capital punishment, 40

capitalism-versus- socialism, 40
Cartesian doubt, 21
causation, problem of, 22–24, 30
Chalmers, David, 77–78
chicken-or-egg dilemma, 9
Church, atrocities of, 31
Church, the, 79
circular reasoning, 14
climate change, 54
*Cogito*, 21, 44–45, 50, 73, 84
conform, 28–29
    education system, 32
consensus, 25–28
conspiracies, 26
Covid-19 virus, 37–38

Darwin, Charles, 36
Darwin, Erasmus, 36
delusional beliefs, 13
denial, 75
Descartes, René, 20–21, 44, 50–51, 73
Devil, temptation by, 80
distance, lacking notion of, 42
Divine Hiddenness Argument, 87
dream, 20, 44, 82, 85–86

Drowning Child thought experiment, 67
dualism, 81–83, 86
Duryodhana, Prince, 60–61
*dweshas*, 71

Einstein, Albert, 32
empiricism, 11
emptying thyself, 44
enlightenment, 57, 87
Enlightenment, the, 13
epistemological nihilism, 19
epistemology, 9–10
euthanasia, 40
evidence
    requirements of, 37
    what is, 37
Evil Demon, 20–21, 74, 87
evolution, 20, 36
evolutionary biology, 32
experience, 10–11, 20

factual relativism, 19
fallibilism, 21, 57
fideism, 66

Genesis (Bible), creation account in, 82
germ theory of disease, 26
ghost in the machine, 86
ghost, perception of, 34–35
global scepticism. 19, 21
God, definition of, 49
God-experience, 57, 87
God's existence
   belief in, 45–46
   philosophical arguments for, 58–59, 66, 69
   the debate on, 45
Goldman, Ron, 38
Gospel of Luke
   ch.17, v.21, 84
Gospel of Matthew
   ch.4, v.1-9, 80
   ch.9, v.17, 55
   ch.13, v.11, 55
   ch.13, vs.13-15, 59
   ch.22, v.37, 66
groupthink, 28

hallucinations, 14–15
Harman, Gilbert, 21
herd mentality, 28, 71
higher knowledge, 18
historical investigation, 75
historical method, 80
Hume, David, 16, 22–23, 30, 76

idealism, 43, 82, 85
ignorance (spiritual), 87
Indian monastic tradition, 70
induction, 21–22, 76
   problem of, 22, 47
   reverse induction, problem of, 76
informational influence, 29, 34
Inquisition, the, 75
internal perception, 15
intuition, 13–14
*Ishvara*, 74
is-ought problem, 16

Jastrow, Joseph, 43
Jesus, 55, 58–60, 66, 80, 84

Kalama Sutta, 61–62
*kama*, 71
Kant, Immanuel, 16, 51

Kierkegaard, Søren, 59
Krishna, 60, 66, 88
Kuhn, Thomas, 30
Kurdi, Alan, 68
Kurukshetra war, 60

Lamarckism, 32
laws of logic, 11, 19, 45, 65
liberation, 57, 87
logic, 11–13
logical empiricism, 13, 53
logical positivism.
   *See* logical empiricism
Longino, Helen, 35–36
Lotus Sutra, ch.16, 59–60
lower knowledge, 18–19, 65
Luther, Martin, 30–31

Mahabharata, 60, 88
materialism, 33, 46, 54, 75–79
   the indoctrination of, 80
McGurk Effect, 41, 47
mental conditioning, 41–43
mental deconditioning, 44
messiahs, 52, 80
metaphysics, 10

methodological naturalism, 75–76
miasma theory of disease, 26
*moha*, 71
*moksha*, 57, 87
monism, 85
moral intuitions, 16
*Moral Law, The* (Sivanesan), 16, 60
morphic resonance, 17
Munchhausen trilemma, 19
mutationism, 32

naturalism, 30, 75–76
neutral monism, 85
New Atheism, 48, 67
Newtonian mechanics, 26
*nirvana*, 56, 87
no-doctrine mind state, 54
non-creationism, 83
non-dualism, 81–83, 85
non-scientific empirical knowledge, 46
normative influence, 29, 34
noumenon, 51

ontology, 9–10
orthogenesis, 32

Pandava brothers, 88
paradigm shifts, 30–33
Pascal, Blaise, 63
   Pascal's Wager, 63–64
peer-review, 33–34
perception, 14
*Philosophers on Philosophy* (Chalmers and Bourget), 76
physicalism, 33, 77–78, 85
policing, 54
politics, bias in, 39
pride, 52
psychiatry, 13, 18, 35, 40
psychological determinism, 74

question begging, 14

rabbit-duck illusion, 42
race science, 27, 37
*ragas*, 71
Ramana Maharishi, Sri, 57
Ranking Theory, 34

rationalism, 12
reason, 11–12
Reformation, 30
religion, bias in, 39
religious indoctrination, 80
revelation, Divine, 51
*rishis*, 63
rope-snake analogy, 81–84
*Rosencrantz and Guildenstern Are Dead* (Stoppard), 34, 47

sages, 63
Sahadeva, 88
saints, 52, 58, 63, 70, 72, 80
*samskaras*, 70, 73
scepticism, 19, 21
science, 11, 21
scientific hypotheses, 17
scientific method, 21, 80
scientism, 11
Self-realisation, 57, 87
Shaw, George Bernard, 63
Sheldrake, Rupert, 17
ships not seen, anecdotes of, 42
*siddhis*, 77, 80
Simpson, O.J., 38

Singer, Peter, 67
snake-rope analogy, 81–84
socialism-versus-capitalism, 40
Socrates, 19, 25, 44, 57
solipsism, 85
soulmate, 16
spiritual aspirants, 70
spiritual determinism, 73–74
Spohn, Wolfgang, 34
spontaneous healings, 77
sport, bias in, 39
*sravana*, 55
Stoppard, Tom, 34
Swami Yogeshwarananda, 54–55, 65, 82–83
syllogism, 12–13
Syria, refugee crisis, 68

theism, 45–46
theological determinism, 74
theory of relativity, 26, 32
touch perception, 15

Upanishads, 18, 81–82
   Chandogya, 51
   Katha, 56, 65

vaccinations, 54
value-free science, 37
*vasanas*, 70, 73
Vedas, 81
veganism, 68
vision (religious experience), 15, 47

walking on water, 77–78
*What do Philosophers Believe* (Chalmers and Bourget), 77–78
white intellectual superiority, 37
Wittgenstein, Ludwig, 43, 53, 57
World War II, 37–38

Yogaswami, 57
*yogis*, 63
Yudhisthira, Prince, 60–61, 88

Zoonomia (Darwin, Erasmus), 36

## Publisher Information

Rowanvale Books provides publishing services to independent authors, writers and poets all over the globe. We deliver a personal, honest and efficient service that allows authors to see their work published, while remaining in control of the process and retaining their creativity. By making publishing services available to authors in a cost-effective and ethical way, we at Rowanvale Books hope to ensure that the local, national and international community benefits from a steady stream of good quality literature.

For more information about us, our authors or our publications, please get in touch.

www.rowanvalebooks.com
info@rowanvalebooks.com

www.ingramcontent.com/pod-product-compliance
Lightning Source LLC
LaVergne TN
LVHW010318070426
835510LV00031B/3449